NEW YORK REVIEW BOOKS
CLASSICS

THE SELECTED POEMS
OF OSIP MANDELSTAM

OSIP MANDELSTAM (1891–1938) was born and raised in St. Petersburg, where he attended the prestigious Tenishev School, before studying at the universities of St. Petersburg and Heidelberg and at the Sorbonne. Mandelstam first published his poems in *Apollyon*, an avant-garde magazine, in 1910, then banded together with Anna Akhmatova and Nicholas Gumilev to form the Acmeist group, which advocated an aesthetic of exact description and chiseled form, as suggested by the title of Mandelstam's first book, *Stone* (1913). During the Russian Revolution, Mandelstam left Leningrad for the Crimea and Georgia, and he settled in Moscow in 1922, where his second collection of poems, *Tristia*, appeared. Unpopular with the Soviet authorities, Mandelstam found it increasingly difficult to publish his poetry, though an edition of collected poems did come out in 1928. In 1934, after reading an epigram denouncing Stalin to friends, Mandelstam was arrested and sent into exile. He wrote furiously during these years, and his wife, Nadezhda, memorized his work in case his notebooks were destroyed or lost. (Nadezhda Mandelstam's extraordinary memoirs of life with her husband, *Hope Against Hope* and *Hope Abandoned*, published in the 1970s, later helped to bring Mandelstam a worldwide audience.) In 1937, Mandelstam's exile ended and he returned to Moscow, but he was arrested again almost immediately. This time he was sentenced to hard labor in Siberia. He was last seen in a transit camp near Vladivostok.

CLARENCE BROWN was born in South Carolina in 1929. He went to Duke, then to the Army Language School (Russian), then to the University of Michigan (Linguistics), and then to Harvard

(Russian Literature). He taught at Princeton until his retirement in 1999. His study of Osip Mandelstam won the Phi Beta Kappa Gauss Award for Criticism. Clarence Brown also served as cartoon editor for the *Saturday Review* and created the comic strip *Ollie*. He now lives in Seattle and writes a newspaper column, "Ink Soup."

W. S. MERWIN was born in New York City in 1927 and grew up in Union City, New Jersey, and in Scranton, Pennsylvania. From 1949 to 1951 he worked as a tutor in France, Portugal, and Majorca. He has since lived in many parts of the world, most recently on Maui in the Hawaiian Islands. He is the author of many books of poems, prose, and translations and has received both the Pulitzer and the Bollingen Prizes for poetry, among numerous other awards.

OSIP MANDELSTAM

SELECTED POEMS

translated by

Clarence Brown

and

W. S. Merwin

NEW YORK REVIEW BOOKS

New York

This is a New York Review Book
Published by The New York Review of Books
1755 Broadway, New York, NY 10019

Library of Congress Cataloging-in-Publication Data
Mandelshtam, Osip, 1891–1938.
  [Poems. English. Selections]
  The selected poems of Osip Mandelstam / translated by Clarence Brown and W. S.
Merwin.
     p. cm. — (New York Review Books classics)
  Includes index.
  ISBN 1-59017-091-1 (pbk. : alk. paper)
  1. Mandelshtam, Osip, 1891–1938—Translations into English. I. Brown,
Clarence, 1929– II. Merwin, W. S. (William Stanley), 1927– III. Mandelshtam,
Osip, 1891–1938. Razgovor o Dante. English. IV. Title. V. Series.
  PG3476.M355A23 2004
  891.71'3—dc22

                              2004014656

ISBN 1-59017-091-1

Printed in the United States of America on acid-free paper.
10 9 8 7 6 5 4 3 2 1

August 2004
www.nyrb.com

CONTENTS

INTRODUCTION

Osip Emilievich Mandelstam was born in Warsaw in January 1891, but his family removed so soon thereafter to the imperial Russian capital, St. Petersburg, that it became, in every meaning of the term save the literal one, his native city. His father was a leather merchant whose ancestors came from Kurland. His mother, born Flora Verblovskaya, was a relative of the famous literary historian Vengerov and prided herself on her family's belonging to the intelligentsia. She herself was a teacher of music, a love of which the most gifted of her three sons inherited. The very fact of their residing in Petersburg testifies to the privileged status of Mandelstam père, for Jews were permitted to do so only exceptionally.

We know little of Osip Mandelstam's childhood aside from what he himself recorded in his autobiographical work *The Noise of Time*. True to its title, it concentrates more on the time than on the young intelligence that was taking it in. But one carries away much more from reading these deliberately blurred and impressionistic pages than a sense of Russia's mauve decade. Writing at a time when there was little left for him to celebrate in the contemporary city, when the very name of Peter's capital had already undergone the change through Petrograd to Leningrad, he celebrated those images and events—the general 'noise' of a culture now dead—that he retained in his mind, and it is from these that we can piece together some notion of his early years. It is a notion made up of contradictions that are unresolved—perhaps unresolvable.

On the one hand there is all the melancholy paraphernalia of the 'dying age'—the 'unhealthy tranquillity and deep provincialism' as Mandelstam put it, and the note of decay is one of the constants of the book; but on the other hand, it is all depicted with such stylistic brio, with such relish for the somehow festive aplomb of Petersburg's going down, accompanied by eternal concerts and military parades as counterpoints to the funeral pomps, that the impression left is that of indelible joy. Upon all of this he knew himself to be looking as an outsider, an onlooker from what he called 'the Judaic chaos' of his family and its traditions:

> But what had I to do with the Guards' festivals, the monotonous prettiness of the host of the infantry and its steeds, the stone-faced battalions flowing with hollow tread down the Millionnaya, gray with marble and granite? All the elegant mirage of Petersburg was merely a dream, a brilliant covering thrown over the abyss, while round about there sprawled the chaos of Judaism—not a motherland, not a house, not a hearth, but precisely a chaos, the unknown womb world whence I had issued, which I feared, about which I made vague conjectures and fled, always fled.

Was it not, then, even more of a triumph that he should so have possessed the Czar's capital and made it his own? Beside such paragraphs one must set the rest of the book: the string of French and Swiss governesses who succeeded one another in the nursery, sedate games in the Summer Garden, the treasures of Russian literature—Pushkin in calico binding and 'heavy' Dostoevsky—as furnished by the family bookcase, the music of Tchaikovsky and Scriabin, concerts by Hofmann and Kubelik, the fine sand of a Finnish summer resort, Vera Komissarzhevskaya's theater, and a richly particular gallery of human portraits. On balance, one's final impression of his childhood is that he spent it savoring experience in an atmosphere that afforded him sufficient emotional security and a certain clarity of self-definition. The contrary assumption would make it more difficult to understand that strength of character that sustained Mandelstam through the tragic years that were to come.

It is a further testimony to his family's standing that he gained admission to the Tenishev School, an academy that managed to be not only thoroughly elite but also doctrinairely 'democratic' and educationally very advanced. Vladimir Nabokov's liberal father would send the future great novelist to the same school some ten years later (to leave memoirs of it predictably different from those of Mandelstam); and another Jew who managed to be admitted, Victor Zhirmunsky, would become one of Russia's greatest scholars and a loyal friend of his classmate Mandelstam for the rest of his life. It was a hotbed of excellence.

From there he went abroad on the first of several trips to study and travel in France, Italy, and Germany. His formal courses during a semester spent at Heidelberg in 1909–1910 included lectures on the philosophy of Kant and on Old French. On his return to Petersburg he entered the University, though he never received his degree. The very fact of his having been accepted as a student was baffling for years, for a Jew could be admitted only with the very highest academic credentials, and though Mandelstam had greatly profited from the Tenishev School, his actual record there was very indifferent. His widow recently revealed that he had undertaken to be baptized a Lutheran somewhere in Finland purely for the sake of being matriculated as a Christian. In later life his attitude toward religion in general and Christianity in particular would have forbidden so lightly considered a step, to which he subsequently attached little importance.

By 1913, the year when *Stone*, his first book of poems, appeared, Mandelstam was already known within the confines of the Petersburg literary world as a poet of unusual promise. Still, the little green brochure struck his contemporaries as a kind of revelation. It was something of a mystery where he had come from. The reigning school was that of Russian Symbolism, which included Alexander Blok, Mandelstam's nearest competitor as Russia's greatest twentieth-century poet, and also Andrey Bely, Valery Bryusov, Konstantine Balmont, Vyacheslav Ivanov, Zinaida Gippius, and a great many others. There is a sense, indeed, in which Symbolism included at one time or another *all* the other poets of Russia's 'Silver Age' on either side of the century mark, for it furnished an indispensable part of their education, and its significance therefore greatly exceeds that of its several successors.

But this brief introduction is hardly the place for polemics, and besides, there are many who find it genuinely consoling to assign individual genius to a multiplicity of 'schools'. Let us stick to the prevailing categories.

Symbolism, then, which had arisen at about the time of Mandelstam's own entrance into the world, was now, on the arrival of his first book, defunct as a unified movement. At the end of the last century it had provided a crash course in poetic re-education after Russian nineteenth-century verse, languishing under the overpowering success of Russian nineteenth-century prose, had seemed at times to aspire to prose itself, or else to retreat into the mere prettiness of numbers. By the end of the first decade of this century, the original Symbolist impulse towards reform of taste and technique had become fragmented and drained off into various neo-Romantic dead-ends such as diabolism, an exaggerated absorption with the ego of the poet, various embarrassing forms of the occult and mystical religion, and, in general, a sort of hankering after the drastic for its own sake. Younger poets coming into their maturity at this time inherited the Symbolist rejuvenation of technique, but their elders' preoccupations in other fields left them cold, and the only other schools of modern Russian poetry that deserve mention along with the Symbolists took their departure. Mayakovsky and Khlebnikov were 'Futurists'. Mandelstam was an 'Acmeist'.

I doubt that the programme of Acmeism, as originally formulated, could ever be arrived at purely by means of induction, on the evidence of the poems alone, for the poets who gathered for a time under its banner were very different one from the other. The leader was Nikolay Gumilev, and the only other poets of any lasting consequence were Gumilev's sometime wife, Anna Akhmatova, and Mandelstam himself. The number of poems by these people which, independently of all overt pronouncements, might reasonably be compared on the basis of their formal and thematic resemblance, so as to evince a distinctly separate movement in poetry, is not large. Put in a few words, the Acmeists' early declarations boil down to a desire for poems free of any Symbolist nonsense about contact with other worlds. Images were to be concrete and sharply realized and the statement of poems rigorously logical. Their strength, like that of Antaeus, was to come from contact with the earth. Gumilev in particular called for a virile, even feral, outlook on life and for a steady, wholesome equilibrium in all things, but especially in the construction of poems. For a notion of what Acmeism was or supposed itself to be, it is tempting to send the English reader to a source much closer to home: Ezra Pound's list of 'Don'ts for Imagists'.

For it is hardly feasible to send him directly to the poems translated here. Indeed, from reading the majority of these poems either in Russian or in English one is more likely to conclude that most of the early tenets of Acmeism had been devised for the express purpose of being ignored by Mandelstam. The fact is that he had his own view of Acmeism, and it is a view that only partly coincides with that outlined above. It also evolved over a long period of time, during which it changed. In 1910 in an essay on François Villon he had already sketched an Acmeist poetic that antedated the later and better known formulations of others. In 1937 Akhmatova reports him as having replied to some heckler demanding a definition of Acmeism that it was 'a homesickness for world culture'. This exhausted, defiant retort was his last word on the subject, but it carries, of course, a good deal more emotional than theoretical weight. In between these dates he found occasions for more extended and reasoned deliberations, the last fully composed of which appears in an essay of 1922, where Mandelstam's Acmeism emerges as half poetics and half moral doctrine. He now called it, revealingly enough, by a new name—the 'organic school'. While it is naturally not possible to treat the full complexity of his thought here, the reader of the following pages will need to know at least this: that the 'logic' so insistently called for by the syndics of the movement has now far more to do with the intuitive and purely verbal logic of inner association—with the logic, say, of Mallarmé—than with the rather commonsense logic of discursive statement to be found in Gumilev. As for the moral component of Mandelstam's Acmeism, that might without undue distortion be put as a kind of democratic humanism, which does not differ greatly from what the Acmeists always, explicitly and by inference, desired.

However one resolves the question whether Acmeism or any other -ism ever existed except on the paper of its manifestoes, it is clear that Acmeists existed, for that is what they were called by themselves and others. They were a group of poets, most of them young and unfledged at the time, who clustered around the commanding personality of Gumilev. When the latter enlisted for the World War, which he did at the first opportunity, he left the group with no natural center, and that was the end of Acmeism in its public and least arguable form—their frequent gatherings to read and discuss their own work. Mandelstam was not conscripted, and of course did not enlist, but he did engage in various home-front activities such as organizing benefit evenings of poetry. *Stone* appeared in a second, expanded edition in 1916.

The deprivations of the War and the Revolution frequently drove Mandelstam to the more tranquil and well-provided south of Russia, especially to the Crimea. Returning to the north at the end of the Civil War, he brought with him a new book, *Tristia*, which was published in 1922. It was the book of a poet who had passed through the schooling of the Symbolists, testified to by the early poems of *Stone*, and the more doctrinaire formulations of primitive Acmeism, to achieve a voice uniquely his own. Mandelstam looked over the heads of his immediate preceptors, as it were, to Derzhavin (1743–1816) and Tyutchev (1803–1873), poets who combine exquisite verbal power with a ceremonious, even oratorical, solemnity of manner. The following year, 1923, both his collections of poetry were brought out in new editions and he was now a poet of considerable and widespread fame. He was also married. His wife, Nadezhda Yakovlevna, is now herself known throughout the world for her moving memoir of their last years together, published in English translation as *Hope Against Hope* (1970). It is chiefly owing to her that our knowledge of Mandelstam's subsequent life is infinitely fuller and more exact than that of his former life.

It became increasingly difficult for him to make a living—not that it had ever been easy. But now the causes were different.

Like practically all the intellectuals of Russia, Mandelstam had welcomed the Revolution, but from a very early time he had also mistrusted the Bolshevik usurpers of it, as had most of the other Acmeists. Gumilev's life had ended before one of the firing squads of the new regime in 1921, and all his former associates were automatically suspect. Employment began to depend more and more upon one's being certifiably loyal, and Mandelstam, who took few pains to conceal his real feelings, was flagrantly not so. Editors of journals and publishing houses were increasingly warned to be on their guard against printing the work of the class enemy. In 1928 Mandelstam published three separate books: *Poems*, which contained his previous two collections plus the poems written between 1921 and 1925; *On Poetry*, his collected critical essays; and *The Egyptian Stamp*, his collected prose. That would make the year seem to be the summit of his career so far, but the appearance is very deceptive. For some three or four years before that he had been forced to live by writing children's books, by doing hack translations and journalism, and by whatever odd jobs he could pick up in the government publishing houses. His standing among connoisseurs of poetry had never been higher, but the Soviet state viewed him with increasing suspicion and malevolence.

In spite of this, he had a very highly placed protector in the person of Nikolay Bukharin, who liked Mandelstam and valued his poetry. It was only through his intervention that Mandelstam survived a plot that was meant to remove him altogether from the profession of letters. In the same year (1928) when three of his own books appeared, Mandelstam brought out Charles de Coster's *Thyl Ulenspiegel*, which he had been commissioned by a government publishing house to edit on the basis of two existing Russian translations. When it appeared, however, Mandelstam's name was printed on the title-page as *translator*. This provided the grounds for a campaign of vilification against him in the press. One of the translators all but accused him of plagiarism, and attacked the editorial work itself as slovenly and inaccurate. To readers in the West this may all seem very small potatoes, but it is necessary to remember, first, that Russian polemics can reach a level of personal invective so outrageous as to be almost literally intolerable, and second, that public defamation of character was only the preliminary step in a series that would end, as Mandelstam foresaw, with his exclusion from the right to publish at all. Furthermore, where his personal honor was concerned, Mandelstam was as touchy as Pushkin. The accusations against him, which were after all merely the public culmination of a long series of private affronts, drove him to paroxysms of rage. Bukharin finally had the campaign stopped and arranged for Mandelstam and his wife to be sent off to distant Armenia, ostensibly for the purpose of reporting on how that country was enjoying sovietization but actually to be out of harm's way. This worked, but the shock of what he had endured during the last years of the Twenties dried up the sources of his poetry for an agonizing period of five years—his 'deaf-mute' period, as he called it. On the way back from Armenia in 1930 he cured himself by a desperate act of self-therapy: a strange and completely unclassifiable work known as *Fourth Prose*. A blend of autobiography, criticism, and sheer excoriation, it is Mandelstam's summation of his defense against all the forces that seemed bent on silencing him. Poetry returned, and so did another work of prose (this one publishable, which in Russia *Fourth Prose* never has been), a work called *Journey to Armenia*. Heavily censored, it appeared in a journal in 1933, the last time that his work would appear in the Soviet press for some three decades of 'non-existence'.

The story of Mandelstam's final years, thanks to his widow's obstinate courage and her own extraordinary powers as a writer, is now widely known. He was arrested in 1934 for having composed a poem in which he made grim fun of Stalin, the 'Kremlin mountaineer', and his relish for torture and execution (see page 69). Someone informed on him and he was immediately clapped into prison, where he underwent intensive interrogation and psychological and physical torment. Friends intervened in so far as they dared or were able—his protector Bukharin was to be among the first victims of Stalin's purge later in the decade—and by some miracle the intervention worked. The poet was not shot, as everyone reasonably supposed that he would be, but exiled, first to a small town in the Urals (where, half insane from the prison experience, he attempted to kill himself) and later on in the provincial town of Voronezh. His wife was at his side from the moment he was put on the train into exile, and her presence literally kept him alive through his remaining years, for his anxiety in her slightest absence was so great as to threaten nervous and physical collapse. They lived on the donations of friends, for the most part. The bouts of mental suffering seem to have been even worse than the physical deprivations; Mandelstam lived in the expectation of imminent peril.

It would be natural to imagine that the poems composed at this period would all be haggard replicas of his experience, but this is not so. There are nightmares of colossal atrocities—'mounds of human heads'—on a scale befitting the actual crimes of Stalin. But the visitations of poetry were occasions far too sustaining and joyous for Mandelstam to derive no more from them than that.

> Opulent poverty, regal indigence!
> Live in it calmly, be at peace.
> Blessed are these days, these nights,
> and innocent is the labor's singing sweetness.

The 'labor' was that of poetry, and in the employment of his art Mandelstam took what, in the light of his circumstances, one is tempted to call an incorrigible delight. There was his favorite bird, the goldfinch, its colors and attitude, to be turned into words, or a boy on a sled, or a Breughel-like winter scene. It was not from mere self-indulgence that his pleasure arose, for Mandelstam, like every Russian poet worthy of the name, felt that his gift imposed upon him an obligation: the people needed poetry no less than bread.

> The people need poetry that will be their own secret
> to keep them awake forever,
> and bathe them in the bright-haired wave
> of its breathing.

The term of exile expired in May 1937, and the Mandelstams returned to Moscow only to find that they had lost the right to 'living-space' upon which Nadezhda had maintained a tenuous hold. Homeless and unable to find work, the following twelve-month is a nightmare of wandering and terror: the wave of second arrests, as they were called, was under way. Mandelstam's condition worsened. He had two heart attacks. Finally, in May 1938, they received the visitors whom they had long expected. Mandelstam's sentence 'for counter-revolutionary activities' was five years of hard labor (he had been seized at a rural sanatorium where he was recuperating). Held for a while in prison, he was put in the autumn on one of the prisoner trains that were then plying between European Russia and its remote eastern regions. He seems to have been quite insane at times, though there were lucid intervals. It must have been during one of these that he wrote a last letter in October, 1938, a scrap of brown paper asking to be sent warm clothes and money and saying that he was being held at a transit camp pending shipment to a permanent one. Alexander Mandelstam received notice that his brother had died—of 'heart failure'—on 27 December 1938.

AN AFTERTHOUGHT ON THE TRANSLATION

It was my intention, and hope, that the foregoing should suffice as a minimal introduction to the poet whose altered voice fills the following pages. The publisher—and, even more cogently, my co-translator—have now convinced me against what may yet prove to have been my better judgment that many readers of such a volume as this will be legitimately curious as to how it came into being. Hence this brief word concerning not so much the voice that was there to be altered, nor yet its altered form, but the process of alteration itself.

For more years than I find it comfortable to admit I have been preparing a study of Mandelstam's life and poetry (now to be published by Cambridge University Press under the title *Mandelstam*), and in the course of that I developed a habit of preparing worksheets on each poem. These included, along with notes on every aspect of the poem that struck me, notations of variant readings, semantic nuances of the diction, peculiarities of the prosody, and so on, a plain English translation, often with numerous alternative translations. Thus, when W. S. Merwin proposed to me in the spring of 1971 that we might collaborate on an English translation of Mandelstam (Russian, by some inadvertance, having been omitted from his impressive array of languages), it struck me that much of my own share of the work had already been done. This proved, though only very partially, to be true, for the first stage in our work was my simply turning over to Merwin my worksheets. From these, with a truly heroic effort of decipherment, he produced first versions. In the intervening couple of years we have, with a pleasure that I trust was mutual, debated the early results, sometimes syllable by syllable, often by painstaking correspondence and more often still by personal meetings in Princeton and London. Bargains were struck, but no compromises were undertaken, I hope, with the English poem that was trying to be born out of Mandelstam's Russian.

The poems that resulted are of course no longer *calques* of the original (though an occasional happy line or two from the worksheet did sometimes survive), but we have not consciously invented thoughts or images that the original could in no sense warrant. It need scarcely be said, I suppose, that we never considered the folly of trying to convey to the ear of our English readers the sounds of the Russian.

Here is an example that will perhaps save much explanation. The beginning of the Russian original of No. 394 might be brought over into a painfully literal English as follows:

Limping automatically [or involuntarily] on the empty earth
with [her] irregular, sweet gait,
she walks, slightly preceding
[her] quick girlfriend and the youth one year older [or
    younger] than she.
The straitened freedom of [her] animating affliction
draws her [on].

And it seems that a lucid surmise
wants to linger in her gait—
[the surmise] that this spring weather
is for us the first mother [i.e., Eve] of the grave's vault
and [that] this will be forever going on.

I am of course unable, and have no desire, to enquire into what
passed through Merwin's mind as he wrestled with something
like the above (and he is, by the way, blameless for this Introduc-
tion), but most literate readers, I think, could account for the
clock that does not occur in Mandelstam's poem. It is a concrete
image (very Mandelstamian, by lucky chance) that *tells* in the
line as one of those limp adverbs would not, and its tick can be
discerned in the *quick* and *back* later on. Why is it her left leg? I
suppose because I told Merwin that the particular verb for limp-
ing normally occurs in a phrase specifying *which* leg is lame, and
I see from the worksheet that I have noted that Natasha Shtempel,
to whom the poem was written in 1937, is in fact lame in her *left*
leg. I spent several delightful days with this now aged lady in
1966 and think I know what Mandelstam meant by 'sweet', but
the word has inconvenient overtones in English—at least for
Merwin. It strikes me that 'drags at her foot' is a marvellous
visual and kinetic image for the rather cerebral sense of the literal
version (there is an entirely different excellence in the Russian,
where the cerebral thought is beautifully concretized by lines
that do not so much describe as *enact* Natasha Shtempel's way of
walking). The repetition of 'she must know' strikes me as
effective in this general context of dire periodicity. There is noth-
ing in the Russian to account for it other than the dire periodicity,
though it occurs to me that my having had to repeat 'surmise'
for the sake of the sense might have helped to prompt it. But it is
pointless to go on praising Merwin's superiority—not over the
original, but over the exiguous sense remaining from it on my
worksheet. One final note: 'go on' results from an altered read-
ing (in the first, now superseded, edition of Vol. 1 of the New
York edition, the Russian word meant 'begin').

Would Mandelstam approve? I cannot quite bring myself up

to the presumption of answering in his name, so I shall rather let him answer for himself by an account of his own practice.

Mandelstam also translated. Like most of the Russian poets who brought about the great reflowering of their art around the turn of the century, he was at home in the languages of culture, and translation was a part of his response to the world. With the advent of the bad times that I have mentioned, when his own work was being systematically rejected by 'vigilant' editors, he was driven to translating in order to live. He had to translate under sweatshop conditions, the texts assigned him being the trash in vogue at the time with the authorities. This loathsome hackwork even crowded out his own muse. He had to endure reading here and there in official reference works, chronicles of the literary scene and so on, that he had given up poetry and 'gone over to translating', a legend that clung to his name for years.

But even under these conditions he sometimes managed to translate in response to the old genuine urgency—out of love. In 1933 he turned four sonnets of Petrarch into Russian. They remained unpublished and indeed unknown until the late Victor Zhirmunsky, his old Tenishev classmate, gave them to me in 1962, whereupon they came out in the New York edition of his works. I had received the texts alone, with no indication of where the originals might be among Petrarch's hundreds of sonnets, so my first concern was naturally to seek these out. It was an awful headache. No sooner would I have identified this or that image in an opening line or two than some wild divergence would convince me that Mandelstam must have been working from another original. The 'other original' stubbornly refusing to turn up, I was driven back to my starting point, and had to conclude what is the point of this little narrative: that Mandelstam had translated Petrarch not into Russian, but into Mandelstam.

Lest any reader think that by lending myself to this undertaking I have switched sides in the Lowell–Nabokov debate, let me say, first, that he should inspect my several tributes to Nabokov, and secondly, that that controversy, now that time had dissipated the fog of animus, can be seen for what it was, a pseudo-controversy. Lowell does not translate into English, but into Lowell; Nabokov can be said to translate into literal English only by those who will accept his definition of literal English: in reality, it is Nabokov. Merwin has translated Mandelstam into Merwin. When one is speaking of writers of the stature of Lowell, Nabokov, and Merwin, this strikes me as being the happiest of situations.

I can imagine, if only just, an English poem that might reproduce what one critic has called the 'cello sound' of this or that poem by Mandelstam or some other of its effects—its rhymes, its plastic sculpture of rhythm, its tenuously resonating change-ringing on some syllabic bell, its abrupt syntactic somersaults, and all the rest. What is more, I can imagine the only audience that might, or should, appreciate this English poem: a roomful of native Russians who, with the original itself unfolding in their mind's ear, have just enough English to collate the two, and approve the result. They would approve it, happily unaware of the exorbitant price that had been paid, and consequently as happily unable to assess its merit as an English poem of our own time.

We have tried to translate Mandelstam into the English that works as an instrument of poetry in our own time, and we have accepted the responsibility entailed in the fact that to translate is to change. Those of my colleagues in the academy who are sent up the wall by 'mistakes' in the translation of poetry, those who are happy to maintain that poetry is untranslatable here on earth, and the arbiters of their own brand of literalism everywhere, have probably by now read far enough in this book.

Clarence Brown
Easter 1973, Princeton

NOTE ON THE TEXT

The Russian text and the numbering of Mandelstam's poems come from his *Sobranie sochinenii* (Collected Works), Vol. I (2nd, ed., revised and expanded, 1967) ed. Gleb Struve and Boris Filippov, with introductions by Clarence Brown, Gleb Struve, and E. M. Rais. New York: Inter-Language Literature Associates.

The poems numbered 92, 112, 113, and 119 were translated by W. S. Merwin and Olga Carlisle and are reprinted from W. S. Merwin, *Selected Translations 1948–1968* (New York, 1968).

FROM *STONE*

The shy speechless sound
of a fruit falling from its tree,
and around it the silent music
of the forest, unbroken . . .   1908

2

Christmas trees burn in the forest with gilded flames,
toy wolves glare from the bushes—

O my prophetic sadness,
O my calm freedom,
and the dead crystal vault of heaven laughing without end!

1908

3

All the lamps were turned low.
You slipped out quickly in a thin shawl.
We disturbed no one.
The servants went on sleeping.   1908

24

Leaves scarcely breathing
in the black breeze;
the flickering swallow
draws circles in the dusk.

In my loving
dying heart
a twilight is coming,
a last ray, gently reproaching.

And over the evening forest
the bronze moon climbs to its place.
Why has the music stopped?
Why is there such silence?   1911

37

THE LUTHERAN

As I was out walking I met a funeral,
last Sunday, by the Lutheran church,
and I stayed idly attending
the stern grief of the faithful.

None of the words of their language came through.
Nothing gleamed but the thin bridles
and the dull glint of the horseshoes, reflected
on the street empty for Sunday.

But in the rocking dusk of the hearse
where the dummy sadness had retired
the autumn roses lay in their buttonhole
without a word or a tear.

Foreigners in black ribbons came walking behind
beside the women weak with weeping,
veils drawn across red faces.
The implacable coachman kept moving on.

Whoever you were, vanished Lutheran
don't worry, it went off well.
The proper tears dimmed the proper eyes,
the right bells rang through the autumn.

And I thought plain thoughts, as was fitting.
We're not prophets nor apostles.
Hell has no fears for us, we repent for no Heaven.
Our candles make a twilight at noon. 1912

47

He can't speak, and we can't bear it!
It's like watching a mutilation of the soul.
A reciter stood on the stage, wild-eyed,
and they went mad, shouting 'Please, please!'

I knew that another was there, invisible,
a man from a nightmare, reading 'Ulalume'.
What's meaning but vanity? A word is a sound—
one of the handmaidens of the seraphim.

Poe's harp-song of the House of Usher. Then the madman
swallowed some water, came to himself, was silent.
I was in the street. The silk of autumn was whistling . . .

1913

'Ulalume': a poem by Edgar Allen Poe (1847).
l.9: the reference is to Poe's short story 'The Fall of the House of Usher' in his
Tales of the Grotesque and Arabesque (1840).

48

THE ADMIRALTY

In the northern capital a dusty poplar languishes.
The translucent clockface is lost in the leaves,
and through the dark green a frigate or acropolis
gleams far away, brother of water and sky.

An aerial ship and a touch-me-not mast,
a yardstick for Peter's successors, teaching
that beauty is no demi-god's whim,
it's the plain carpenter's fierce rule-of-eye.

The four sovereign elements smile on us,
but man in his freedom has made a fifth.
Do not the chaste lines of this ark
deny the dominion of space?

The capricious jellyfish clutch in anger,
anchors are rusting like abandoned plows—
and behold the locks of the three dimensions are sprung
and all the seas of the world lie open.   1913

54

Poison in the bread, the air drunk dry.
Hard to doctor the wounds.
Joseph sold into Egypt
grieved no more bitterly for home.

Bedouins under the stars
close their eyes, sitting their horses,
and improvise songs
out of the troubles of the day.

No lack of subject:
one lost a quiver in the sand,
one bartered away a stallion . . .
the mist of events drifts away.

And if the song is sung truly,
from the whole heart, everything
at last vanishes: nothing is left
but space, the stars, the singer.   1913

60

The horse-shoes still ring
with the old days.
The doormen sleep on the counters
like bales of furs.

And the porter, weary as a king,
hears knocking at the iron gate,
gets up yawning like a barnyard—
they've waked the old Scythian!

So Ovid with his waning love
wove Rome with snow in his lines,
and sang of the ox-cart
in our wild wagon-trains.   1914

62

Orioles in the woods: length of vowels alone
makes the meter of the classic lines. No more
than once a year, though, nature pours out
the full-drawn length, the verse of Homer.

This day yawns like a caesura: a lull
beginning in the morning, difficult, going on and on:
the grazing oxen, the golden langor powerless
to call out of the reed the riches of one whole note.

1914

Let the names of imperial cities
caress the ears with brief meaning.
It's not Rome the city that lives on,
it's man's place in the universe.

Emperors try to rule that,
priests find excuses for wars,
but the day that place falls empty
houses and altars are trash.   [1914]

Insomnia. Homer. Taut sails.
I've read to the middle of the list of ships:
the strung-out flock, the stream of cranes
that once rose above Hellas.

Flight of cranes crossing strange borders,
leaders drenched with the foam of the gods,
where are you sailing? What would Troy be to you,
men of Achaea, without Helen?

The sea—Homer—it's all moved by love. But to whom
shall I listen? No sound now from Homer,
and the black sea roars like a speech
and thunders up the bed.   1915

The old ewes, the black Chaldeans,
the spawn of night, cowled in darkness,
go off grumbling to the hills
like plebs annoyed at Rome,

in thousands, shuffling their
knees shaggy as bird-perches,
shaking and bounding in their foaming curls
like lots in a giant wheel.

They need their Caesar. They need their black hill,
the Rome of the sheep, with its seven hills,
and the barking of dogs, a campfire under the sky,
and the rank smoke of a hut and barn.

The bushes marched at them like a wall.
The tents of the warriors started to run.
They left in holy disorder.
The fleece hangs in a heavy wave.   [1915]

80

Herds of horses neigh happily in the meadows
and the valley has rusted as Rome did.
The transparent river bears away
dry gold: the spring days of the classics.

In autumn, in the wilderness, trampling
the oak leaves that have buried the paths,
I remember Caesar, the imperial features
like a woman's, from the side, with the nose of one
                                    not to be trusted.

Capitol, Forum, are far away
from these colors draining peacefully out of the season.
Even on the rim of the world I can hear the time
of Augustus rolling away, an orb, an apple.

When I'm old, may even my sadness shine.
In Rome I was born, and it comes back to me.
My she-wolf was kind autumn,
And August smiled on me—the month of the Caesars.

1915

FROM *TRISTIA*

How these veils and these shining robes
weigh me down in my shame!

A famous disaster
is coming to stone Troezen,
the royal stairs
will be scarlet with shame.

. . . .

. . . .

and a black sun will rise
to light the mother's desire.

If it were only hatred that seethed in me—
but look, the truth opened its wings and left me.

Phaedra the black flame is burning
by day,
a torch for a death, for a burial
by day.
Hippolytus, beware of your mother:
Phaedra is the night watching you
by day.

I have stained the sun with my black love.
Pure death will be cold to the lips.

We are afraid. A queen
and we are afraid to grieve.
Goaded by Theseus,
the night struck him down,
and we are a dirge
going home with the dead
to chill the black sun
that raged and would not sleep.   1916

The two lines deleted by Mandelstam (indicated here by rows of dots) were
never restored.

to Marina Tsvetaeva

On a sled covered with straw.
Our own matting scarcely covered us.
We rode through wide Moscow
from the Sparrow Hills to a little church we knew well.

Children in Uglich play at knucklebones.
A smell of bread baking.
I am taken through streets bare-headed.
In the chapel three lighted candles.

Not three lights but three meetings,
one blessed by God himself.
There will be no fourth. Rome is far.
And He never loved it.

The sled drove along black ruts.
People coming back from their walks.
Thin muzhiks and cross old women
restless at the gate.

In the raw distance a night of birds rose.
The bound hands went numb.
They're bringing the Tsarevich. The body turns to ice.
They set fire to the straw.

1916

Marina Tsvetaeva (1892–1941), one of the greatest of modern Russian poets, left
Russia after the Revolution but returned in 1939 and hanged herself two years
later. She and Mandelstam were close for a time in 1916.
l.5: Dimitry, son of Ivan IV and rightful heir to the throne of Muscovy, was
killed in the town of Uglich. Boris Godunov was suspected of complicity.

SOLOMINKA

I

Solominka, when you can't sleep in the huge chamber,
when you lie awake under the steep ceiling
waiting for its indifference to descend
onto your eyelids that feel everything,

dry Solominka, little ringing straw
who sipped up the whole of death—it has made you gentle.
The little dead straw has broken. It was Solominka.
No, not Salomea. It was the dead one.

Sleep won't come, but things grow heavier.
There are less of them than there were. And what silence!
The pillows hardly show in the mirror.
The bed floats on a lake, on a glass.

But that's not Solominka, under the grave satin,
above the black Neva, in the huge chamber.
The twelve months are singing of the hour of death
and the blue air is a river pale with ice.

The breath of grave December is flowing.
The room fills with the whole weight of the Neva.
It's not Solominka, it's Ligeia, dying.
I have learned you, blessed words.

II

I have learned you, blessed words.
Lenore, Solominka, Ligeia, Seraphita.
The huge room is full of the whole weight of the Neva.
Blood runs pale-blue from the granite.

Grave December gleams above the Neva.
The twelve months sing of the hour of death.
No, that's not Solominka, under the grave satin,
the dry straw sipping the deadly peace.

In my blood Ligeia is December.
Her blessed voice is asleep in the lidded stone.
But pity killed Solominka—or Salomea.
Whichever it was will never return.   1916

The name Solominka is also the Russian word for 'a straw'.
stanza 6: Lenore is one of the pale maidens of Edgar Allen Poe (see 'The Raven'),
as is Ligeia (see the story of that name). Séraphita is the heroine (and sometimes
the hero) of Balzac's novel by that name, 1835. Salomea is the name of the
addressee of this poem, Princess Salomea Andronikova. For a full analysis of this
poem see Clarence Brown, *Mandelstam* (Cambridge University Press, 1973), pp.
237–44.

89

We shall die in transparent Petropolis,
before Persephone our queen.
When we sigh we swallow the air of death.
Every hour will commemorate our last moments.

Sea-goddess, stern Athena,
lift off your great stone helmet.
We shall die in transparent Petropolis,
where Persephone, not you, is the queen.   1916

l.1: Mandelstam, like some other poets (e.g. Derzhavin), occasionally refers to
St. Petersburg as Petropolis—'the city of Peter'.

90

With no faith in the miracle of resurrection
we wandered through the cemetery.
—You know, everywhere
the earth reminds me of those hills

. . . .
. . . .
where Russia breaks off
above the black desolate sea.

16

A wide meadow falls away
under the monastery.
I wanted to stay in the plains
of Vladimir, and not go south,
but to linger in that dark wooden
colony of holy fools
with that foggy nun
was to wall myself up in trouble.

I kiss your sunburnt elbow
and a place on your wan forehead
which I know has stayed white
under the strand of dark gold.
I kiss your hand, the white
band the bracelet left.
The blazing summer of Taurida
performs miracles such as these.

How quickly you tanned,
and came to the Savior's poor icon,
and kissed without stopping,
you who were proud in Moscow.
The name is all that's left to us,
a miraculous sound.
Here, take this sand that I pour
from one palm to another.   1916

Mandelstam never added the lines indicated here as missing.

91

BLACK SUN

Nothing can erase this night
but there's still light with you.
At Jerusalem's gate
a black sun has risen.

The yellow one frightens me more.
Lullaby, lullaby. Israelites
have buried my mother
in the bright temple.

Somewhere outside grace,
with no priests to lead them,
Israelites have sung the requiem over her
in the bright temple.

The voices of Israelites
rang out over my mother.
I woke in the cradle, dazzled
by the black sun.   1916

92

The thread of gold cordial flowed from the bottle
with such languor that the hostess found time to say
here in mournful Tauris where our fates have cast us
we are never bored—with a glance over her shoulder.

On all hands the rites of Bacchus, as though the whole world
held only guards and dogs. As you go you see no one.
And the placid days roll past like heavy barrels. Far off
in the ancient rooms there are voices. Can't make them out.
    Can't answer.

After tea we went out into the great brown garden.
Dark blinds are dropped like eyelashes on the windows.
We move along the white columns looking at grapes. Beyond
    them
airy glass has been poured over the drowsing mountains.

I said the grape vines live on like an antique battle,
with gnarled cavalry tangling in curving waves.
Here in stone-starred Tauris is an art of Hellas: here, rusted,
are the noble ranks of the golden acres.

Meanwhile silence stands in the white room like a spinning
    wheel,
smelling of vinegar, paint, wine cool from the cellar.
Do you remember in the Greek house the wife they all loved?
Not Helen. The other. And how long she embroidered?

Golden fleece, where are you then, golden fleece?
All the way the heaved weight of the sea rumbled.
Leaving his boat and its sea-wearied sails,
Odysseus returned, filled with space and time.   1917

93

Far away is the gray
transparent spring of asphodels.
For the moment the sand still rustles,
in fact, the wave still seethes.
But here, like Persephone, my soul
enters the fortunate circle.
Such beautiful sunburnt hands as these
are not found in the kingdom of Hades.

Why do we entrust to a boat
the weight of the funeral urn,
and perform the black rose rite
over the amethyst water?
To the sea past Cape Meganom,
through the fogs, my soul is fighting;
a black sail will come back from there
after the burial.

How fast the unlighted bank
of storm clouds passes,
and under this windy moon
black rose petals are flying.
And that bird of death and grief,
the huge flag, memory,
trails from the cypress stern
a black border.

The sad fan of the past
opens with a hiss, toward the place
where the amulet was buried,
with a dark shudder, in the sand.
To the sea past Cape Meganom,
through the fogs, my soul is fighting;
a black sail will come back from there
after the burial.   1917

96

A hush that evening in the organ forest.
Then singing for us: Schubert, cradle songs,
the noise of a mill, and the voice of a storm
where the music had blue eyes and was drunk and laughing.

Brown and green is the world of the old song,
and young forever. There the maddened king
of the forest shakes the whispering crowns
of the nightingale lindens.

With darkness he returns, and his terrible strength
is wild in that song, like a black wine.
He is the Double, an empty ghost
peering mindlessly through a cold window.   1917

The clock-cricket singing,
that's the fever rustling.
The dry stove hissing,
that's the fire in red silk.

The teeth of mice milling
the thin supports of life,
that's the swallow my daughter
who unmoored my boat.

Rain-mumble on the roof—
that's the fire in black silk.
But even at the bottom of the sea
the bird-cherry will hear 'good-bye'.

For death is innocent,
and the heart,
all through the nightingale-fever,
however it turns, is still warm.   1917

101

A wandering fire at a terrible height—
can it be a star shining like that?
Transparent star, wandering fire,
your brother, Petropolis, is dying.

The dreams of earth blaze at a terrible height,
a green star is burning.
O if you are a star, this brother of water and sky,
your brother, Petropolis, is dying.

A giant ship at a terrible height
is rushing on, spreading its wings.
Green star, in splendid poverty
your brother, Petropolis, is dying.

Above the black Neva transparent spring
has broken, the wax of immortality is melting.
O if you are a star, Petropolis, your city,
your brother, Petropolis, is dying.   1918

103

THE TWILIGHT OF FREEDOM

Let us praise the twilight of freedom, brothers,
the great year of twilight!
A thick forest of nets has been let down
into the seething waters of night.
O sun, judge, people, desolate
are the years into which you are rising!

Let us praise the momentous burden
that the people's leader assumes, in tears.
Let us praise the twilight burden of power,
its weight too great to be borne.
Time, whoever has a heart
will hear your ship going down.

We have roped swallows together
into legions.
Now we can't see the sun.
Everywhere nature twitters as it moves.
In the deepening twilight the earth swims into the nets
and the sun can't be seen.

But what can we lose if we try one
groaning, wide, ungainly sweep of the rudder?
The earth swims. Courage,
brothers, as the cleft sea falls back from our plow.
Even as we freeze in Lethe we'll remember
the ten heavens the earth cost us.

Moscow. May 1918

TRISTIA

I have studied the science of good-byes,
the bare-headed laments of night.
The waiting lengthens as the oxen chew.
In the town the last hour of the watch.
And I have bowed to the knell of night in the rooster's throat
when eyes red with crying picked up their burden
of sorrow and looked into the distance
and the crying of women and the Muses' song became one.

Who can tell from the sound of the word 'parting'
what kind of bereavements await us,
what the rooster promises with his loud surprise
when a light shows in the Acropolis,
dawn of a new life,
the ox still swinging his jaw in the outer passage,
or why the rooster, announcing the new life,
flaps his wings on the ramparts?

A thing I love is the action of spinning:
the shuttle fluttering back and forth, the hum of the spindle,
and look, like swan's down floating toward us,
Delia, the barefoot shepherdess, flying—
o indigence at the root of our lives,
how poor is the language of happiness!
Everything's happened before and will happen again,
but still the moment of each meeting is sweet.

Amen. The little transparent figure
lies on the clean earthen plate
like a squirrel skin being stretched.
A girl bends to study the wax.
Who are we to guess at the hell of the Greeks?
Wax for women, bronze for men:
our lot falls to us in the field, fighting,
but to them death comes as they tell fortunes.   1918

l.20: Delia is a traditional name for the enamored shepherdess of pastoral poems.
The name occurs a few times in some of Pushkin's early lyrics.

108

Heaviness and tenderness—sisters: the same features.
Bees and wasps suck the heavy rose.
Man dies, heat leaves the sand, the sun
of yesterday is borne on a black stretcher.

Oh the heavy honeycomb, the tender webs—easier
to hoist a stone than to say your name!
Only one purpose is left me, but it is golden:
to free myself of the burden, time.

I drink the roiled air like a dark water.
Time has been plowed; the rose was earth. In a slow
whirlpool the heavy tender roses,
rose heaviness, rose tenderness, are plaited in double wreaths.
                                        Koktebel. March 1920

Venice, the stagnant, barren life—
it's plain what it means.
Look at it, peering with its cold smile
into the blue decayed glass.

Faint scent of leather. Fine veins in blue ink.
White snow. Green brocade.
They ride in cypress sedan chairs
and emerge from their cloaks, warm and dozing.

And candles still burn, burn, in baskets:
as if the dove had flown back into the Ark.
And on stage and among the listless assembly
man is dying.

For there's no way out of love and terror:
the ring of Saturn is heavier than platinum.
The block is draped in black velvet
and so is the beautiful face.

O Venice, the weight of your garments
and of your mirrors in their cypress frames!
Your air is cut in facets, and mountains
of blue decayed glass melt in the bedchamber.

A rose or a phial between fingers—
green Adriatic, farewell!
Why are you silent? Lady of Venice,
how can one escape this festivity of death?

The evening star flashes black in the mirror.
Everything passes. Truth is dark.
Man is born. Pearl dies.
Susanna will have to wait for the elders.   1920

FEODOSIA

In the ring of high hills
you stampede down your slope like sheep,
pink and white stones glistening
in the dry transparent air.
Pirate feluccas rock out at sea.
The port burns with poppies—Turkish flags.
Reed masts. The wave's resilient crystal.
Little boats on ropes like hammocks.

From morning till night, in every way possible,
everyone sings, grieving for a 'little apple'.
Its golden seed is borne away by the wind
and lost, and will never come back.
And promptly at nightfall, in the lanes,
the musicians, in twos and threes
bend and clumsily scrape
their improbable variations.

O little statues of Roman-nosed pilgrims!
O joyful Mediterranean bestiary!
Turks strut about in towels,
like roosters, by little hotels.
Dogs are moved in a small jail on wheels.
Dry dust blows in the streets,
and the vast cook from the battleship
looms cold-blooded above the market Furies.

Let's go where they've a collection of sciences,
and the art of making *shashlyk* and *chebureki*,
where the sign shows a pair of pants
to tell us what a man is.
A man's long coat, working without a head,
a barber's flying violin,
a hypnotized iron, a vision of heavenly
laundresses, smiling because it's difficult.

Here girls grow old in bangs
and ponder their curious garments.
Admirals in three-cornered hats
bring back Scheherazade's dream.
Transparent distance. A few grapevines.
A fresh wind that never drops.
And it's not far to Smyrna and Baghdad,
but it's a hard sail, and the same stars everywhere.

1920

112

When Psyche, who is Life, steps down into the shadows,
the translucent wood, following Persephone,
a blind swallow casts itself at her feet
with Stygian tenderness and a green branch.

The shades swarm to welcome the refugee,
their new little companion, and greet her with eager wailing,
wringing their frail arms before her
in awe and trouble and shy hope.

One of them holds out a mirror, and another, perfume,
because the soul is a woman and fond of trifles.
And the silence of the leafless forest is spotted
with transparent voices, dry laments, like a fine rain.

And in the fond confusion, uncertain where to begin,
the soul does not recognize the transparent woods.
She breathes on the mirror and she still clutches
the copper wafer, the fee for the misty crossing.   1920

I have forgotten the word I wanted to say.
A blind swallow returns to the palace of shadows
on clipped wings to flicker among the Transparent Ones.
In oblivion they are singing the night song.

No sound from the birds. No flowers on the immortelles.
The horses of night have transparent manes.
A little boat drifts on the dry river.
Among the crickets the word fades into oblivion.

And it rises slowly like a pavilion or a temple,
performs the madness of Antigone,
or falls at one's feet, a dead swallow,
with Stygian tenderness and a green branch.

Oh to bring back also the shyness of clairvoyant
fingers, the swelling joy of recognition.
I shrink from the wild grieving of the Muses,
from the mists, the ringing, the opening void.

It is given to mortals to love, to recognize,
to make sounds move to their fingers,
but I have forgotten what I wanted to say
and a bodiless thought returns to the palace of shadows.

The Transparent One still speaks, but of nothing.
Still a swallow, a friend known as a girl, Antigone.
The reverberations of Stygian remembrance
burn like black ice on one's lips.   November 1920

On the stage of ghosts a pale gleaming:
faint choirs of shades.
Melpomene has smothered the windows
of her house with silk.
Out in the courtyard the black camp
of carriages crackles with frost.
Long furs, everything shaggy,
hot snow sounding of teeth.

Servants sort bearskin coats
one by one from the piles.
One moth flies above many hands.
There's a rose under the furs.
Tiers of glittering fashionable insects
rise in the heat of the theater.
Out in the street little lights
flicker. Billows of steam roll in.

The coachmen have shouted themselves tired.
The crowd puffs and snores.
Ours is a cold winter, dear Eurydice.
Never mind. Sweeter to me
than the singing speech of Italy
is the language to which I was born.
Notes of remote harps well up in it
in secret.

Smoke hangs in the ragged sheepskins.
The street's black with drifted snow.
Out of the blessed singing height
immortal spring is flying to us
with the deathless aria:
—You will see green fields again;
the living swallow fell
on hot snow.   1920

l.3: Melpomene is the muse of tragedy.

Take from my palms, to soothe your heart,
a little honey, a little sun,
in obedience to Persephone's bees.

You can't untie a boat that was never moored,
nor hear a shadow in its furs,
nor move through thick life without fear.

For us, all that's left is kisses
tattered as the little bees
that die when they leave the hive.

Deep in the transparent night they're still humming,
at home in the dark wood on the mountain,
in the mint and lungwort and the past.

But lay to your heart my rough gift,
this unlovely dry necklace of dead bees
that once made a sun out of honey.   November 1920

There: the Eucharist, a gold sun,
hung in the air—an instant of splendor.
Here nothing should be heard but the Greek syllables—
the whole world held in the hands like a plain apple.

The solemn height of the holy office; the light
of July in the rotunda under the cupola;
so that we may sigh from full hearts, outside time,
for that little meadow where time does not flow.

And the Eucharist spreads like an eternal noon;
all partake of it, everyone plays and sings,
and in each one's eyes the sacred vessel
brims over with inexhaustible joy.   [1920]

We shall meet again, in Petersburg,
as though we had buried the sun there,
and then we shall pronounce for the first time
the blessed word with no meaning.
In the Soviet night, in the velvet dark,
in the black velvet Void, the loved eyes
of blessed women are still singing,
flowers are blooming that will never die.

The capital hunches like a wild cat,
a patrol is stationed on the bridge,
a single car rushes past in the dark,
snarling, hooting like a cuckoo.
For this night I need no pass.
I'm not afraid of the sentries.
I will pray in the Soviet night
for the blessed word with no meaning.

A rustling, as in a theater,
and a girl suddenly crying out,
and the arms of Cypris are weighed down
with roses that will never fall.
For something to do we warm ourselves at a bonfire,
maybe the ages will die away
and the loved hands of blessed women
will brush the light ashes together.

Somewhere audiences of red flowers exist,
and the fat sofas of the loges,
and a clockwork officer
looking down on the world.
Never mind if our candles go out
in the velvet, in the black Void. The bowed shoulders
of the blessed women are still singing.
You'll never notice the night's sun.

25 November 1920

I could not keep your hands in my own,
I failed the salt tender lips,
so I must wait now for dawn in the timbered Acropolis.
How I loathe the ageing stockades and their tears.

The Achaeans are constructing the horse in the dark,
hacking out the sides with their dented saws.
Nothing quiets the blood's dry fever, and for you
there is no designation, no sound, no modelled likeness.

How did I dare to think you might come back?
Why did I tear myself from you before it was time?
The dark has not faded yet, nor the cock crowed,
nor the hot axe bitten wood.

Resin has seeped from the stockade like transparent tears
and the town is conscious of its own wooden ribs,
but blood has rushed to the stairs and started climbing
and in dreams three times men have seen the seductive image.

Where is Troy, the beloved? The royal, the queenly roof.
Priam's high bird house will be hurled down
while arrows rattle like dry rain
and grow from the ground like shoots of a hazel.

The pin-prick of the last star vanishes without pain,
morning will tap at the shutter, a gray swallow,
and the slow day, like an ox that wakes on straw,
will lumber out from its long sleep to cross the rough haycocks.

December 1920

At the hour when the moon appears in its city
and the wide avenues slowly fill with its light
then the night swells with bronze and sadness,
time the barbarian smashes the wax songs,

then the cuckoo counts her griefs on the stone tower
and the pale woman with the sickle steps down
through the dead, scattering straw on the board floor,
rolling huge spokes of shadow slowly across it.   1920

122

Let me be in your service
like the others
mumbling predictions,
mouth dry with jealousy.
Parched tongue
thirsting, not even for the word—
for me the dry air is empty
again without you.

I'm not jealous any more
but I want you.
I carry myself like a victim
to the hangman.
I will not call you
either joy or love.
All my own blood is gone.
Something strange paces there now.

Another moment
and I will tell you:
it's not joy but torture
you give me.
I'm drawn to you
as to a crime—
to your ragged mouth,
to the soft bitten cherry.

Come back to me,
I'm frightened without you.
Never had you such power
over me as now.
Everything I desire
appears to me.
I'm not jealous any more.
I'm calling you.   1920

123

A ring of shades danced on the springing meadow.
I threw among them a name like a song.
Everything melted. Only a mist
of sound remained with me.

I thought first that the name was one of the seraphim,
I was shy of bodies however light.
A few days and we flowed together;
I melted into a beloved shade.

Wild fruit falls again from the apple tree
and the image drifts by me like mist,
with curses for heaven and for itself,
still swallowing embers of jealousy.

And happiness rolls on like a gold hoop
someone else is guiding.
Spring drifts away and you chase it
waving your hand like a knife.

As it is we never emerge from the dance,
from the ring, from the enchantment.
Earth, the virgin, springs up again
in hills, but the mist hides them from us.   1920

FROM *POEMS* (1928)

CONCERT AT THE RAILWAY STATION

Can't breathe. And the firmament seething with worms,
and not one star speaking.
But as God's our witness, there's music above us—
the Aeonian maids, at whose song the station trembles,
and again the violin-laden air is sundered
and fused together by the whistles of trains.

Immense park. The station a glass sphere.
A spell cast again on the iron world.
The train carriage is borne away in state
to the echoing feast in misty Elysium.
Peacocks crying, a piano's bass notes—
I'm late. I'm afraid. This is a dream.

And I enter the station, the glass forest.
The harmony of violins is dishevelled and weeping.
The savage life of the night choir,
a smell of roses from rotting beds,
where the beloved shade passed the night
under the glass sky, among the travelling crowds.

And I think, how like a beggar the iron world
shivers, covered with music and froth.
And I go out through the glass passage. The steam
blinds the pupils of the violin bows. Where are you off to?
It's the funeral feast of the beloved shade.
It's the last time the music sounds for us.   1921

I was washing outside in the darkness,
the sky burning with rough stars,
and the starlight, salt on an axe-blade.
The cold overflows the barrel.

The gate's locked,
the land's grim as its conscience.
I don't think they'll find the new weaving,
finer than truth, anywhere.

Star-salt is melting in the barrel,
icy water is turning blacker,
death's growing purer, misfortune saltier,
the earth's moving nearer to truth and to dread.   1921

To some winter is nut-stains and blue-eyed punch,
to some, wine fragrant with cinnamon, and to some
it's a salt of commands from the cruel stars
to carry into a smoky hut.

The warm droppings of a few hens
and a tepid muddle of sheep.
For life, for life and care, I'll give up everything.
A kitchen match could keep me warm.

Look, all I have with me is a clay pot
and the twitterings of the stars in my thin ears.
I can't help loving through unfledged bird skin
the yellow of grass, warmth of the black earth.

To smoothe out fur and turn straw in silence,
and hunger like an apple tree wrapped against winter,
stupidly, and thirst for another
and touch nothing in the dark, and wait.

Well may the conspirators hurry over the frail
creaking snow-crust like a flock of sheep. To some, winter
is wormwood, and bitter smoke as the tents are pitched,
to others, a sheet of salt ready to fall.

O if I could hoist a lantern on a long pole
and be led by a dog, under the salt of stars,
with a rooster in a pot, to the fortune-teller's yard.
But the white of the snow eats the eyes to the quick.   1922

129

The scalp tingles with cold.
Nobody speaks out.
Time pares me away
like the heel of your shoe.

Life overcomes life.
The sound fades out.
Something is always missing.
There's no time to remember it.

You know, it was better before.
But there's no comparing
how the blood used to whisper
and how it whispers.

It's plain that some purpose
is moving these lips.
The tree-top laughs and plays
into the day of the axes.   1922

No way of knowing
when this song began.
Does the thief rustle to its tune? ....
Does the prince of mosquitoes hum it?

O, if I could speak once more
about nothing at all,
blaze up like a struck match,
nudge night awake with my shoulder,

heave up the smothering haystack,
the muffling hat of air,
shake out the stitches
of the sack of caraway seeds,

then the pink knot of blood,
the hushing of these dry grasses
would be here in their trance after
a century, a hayloft, a dream.   1922

I climbed the ladder leaning against the hay,
into the uncombed loft.
I breathed the haydust of milky stars.
I breathed the matted scurf of space.

And I thought, why stir up the swarm
of long drawn-out lines of sound?
Why imprison the miraculous Aeolian harmony
in this ceaseless squabble?

The Great Bear, the dipper, has seven stars.
On earth there are five good senses.
The darkness swells and rings out,
and swells and rings out again.

The huge unhitched load sticks up
on top of the universe,
and soon the hayloft, the old chaos,
will itch and swirl with dust.

We rustle fish-scales that are not ours.
We sing against the fur of the world.
We string a lyre, as though we could not wait
for the shaggy fleece to grow over us.

Mowers bring back the goldfinches
that have fallen from their nests.
I will burst out of these burning lines
and return to the phrase of sound where I was born,

so that the pink link of blood
and the one-armed ringing of the grass may pronounce
their last good-byes: the one mustering courage,
the other setting out for its dream beyond reason.   1922

133

The wind brought comfort to us.
We could feel in the azure
dragonflies with Assyrian wings,
vibrations of the noded dark.

And the darkened sky's underside
threatened like the thunder of armies,
forest of mica membranes
flying with six-armed bodies.

There is a blind niche in the azure:
in each blessed noon
one fateful star trembles,
hinting at the depth of night.

And Azrael, among scales of crippled wings
threading his difficult way,
takes by its high arm
the defeated sky.   1922

l.13: Azrael, in Jewish and Mohammedan angelology, is the angel of death.

135

THE AGE

My animal, my age, who will ever be able
to look into your eyes?
Who will ever glue back together the vertebrae
of two centuries with his blood?
Blood the maker gushes
from the throats of the things of earth.
Already the hanger-on is trembling
on the sills of days to come.

Blood the maker gushes
from the throats of the things of earth
and flings onto a beach like a burning fish
a hot sand of sea-bones,
and down from the high bird-net,
out of the wet blocks of sky
it pours, pours, heedlessly
over your death-wound.

Only a metal the flute has melted
will link up the strings of days
until a time is torn out of jail
and the world starts new.
The age is rocking the wave
with human grief
to a golden beat, and an adder
is breathing in time with it in the grass.

The buds will go on swelling,
the rush of green will explode,
but your spine has been shattered,
my splendid derelict, my age.
Cruel and feeble, you'll look back
with the smile of a half-wit:
an animal that could run once,
staring at his own tracks.   1923

The original second stanza of this poem was cancelled by Mandelstam and
replaced by the lines that serve as the basis of this translation on 3 February
1936—C.B.

136

HE WHO FINDS A HORSESHOE

We look at the forest and we say
here are many ships already in the trees, masts,
the red pines
bare of their rough burden clear to the top,
they should creak in the storm
like solitary pines,
in the raging treeless air.
The plumbline fixed
to the dancing deck, under the wind's salt heel,
will hold fast, as the sea-farer,
with unbridled thirst for distance, trawls
through the furrows of water the geometer's
frail instruments, tracing
against the pull of the bosom of the earth
the rough surfaces of the seas.

And breathing the smell of the tears
of resin that seep from the ship's timbers,
gazing lovingly upon
the rivetted boards fitted into bulkheads
(not by the peaceable Bethlehem carpenter
but by that other, the father
of wanderings, the sea-farer's friend)
we say
these too once stood on the earth,
uncomfortable as a donkey's spine,
their tops forgetting their roots,
on a famous mountain,
and sighed under the sweet pouring rain,
and in vain offered to heaven their noble burden
for a pinch of salt.

Where to start?
Everything cracks and shakes.
The air trembles with similes.
No one word's better than another;
the earth moans with metaphors,
and the shays hitched to shimmering flocks
of birds all heaving together
fly apart, racing
against the day's favorites.

Thrice blessed is he who puts a name in his song.
The song graced with a name
outlives the others.
She may be known among her companions by her headband
that preserves her from fainting, from too-strong numbing
    odors
whether of the nearness of man,
the fur of a powerful animal, or simply
the smell of savory rubbed between hands.

Sometimes the air is dark as water, and everything in it
is swimming like a fish,
fanning its way through the sphere,
through the dense, yielding, scarcely warm
crystal with wheels moving in it, and horses shying,
and Neaera's damp black earth, that is turned up afresh
every night by forks, tridents, mattocks, plows.
The air is as deeply mingled as the earth;
you can't get out of it, and it's hard to get in.

A rustling runs through the trees as through a lush meadow.
Children play jacks with bits of animals' backbones.
The frail tally of our age is almost done.
For what there was, thank you.
For my part, I made mistakes, got lost,
came out wrong. The age clanged like a golden ball,
hollow, seamless, held by no one.
When it was touched it answered 'yes' and 'no'
as a child answers
'I'll give you the apple', or 'I won't give you the apple',
with a face that matches the voice saying the words.

The sound is still ringing, though what caused it has gone.
The stallion is lying in a lather, in the dust, snorting,
but the tight arch of his neck recalls
the stretched legs racing,
not just the four of them
but as many as the stones on the road
coming alive by fours
at each bound of the fiery pacer.

Therefore
the one who finds a horseshoe
blows the dust from it,
rubs it with wool till it shines,
and then
hangs it over the door
to rest,
not to be made to strike sparks from the flint again.
Human lips
        that have no more to say
keep the shape of the last word they said,
and the hand goes on feeling the full weight
even after the jug
        has splashed itself half empty
                        on the way home.

What I'm saying now isn't said by me.
It's dug out of the ground like grains of petrified wheat.
Some portray
        a lion on their coins,
others
        a head;
all sorts of round bits of brass, gold, bronze
lie in the earth sharing the same honor.
The age tried to bite through them, leaving its teethmarks.
Time gnaws at me like a coin,
and there's not even enough of me left for myself.

                                    Moscow. 1923

l.53: Neaera is a name often used by classical poets for 'sweetheart'. Cf. Milton's
'the tangles of Neaera's hair' in *Lycidas*.

THE SLATE ODE

Two stars coming together—a great meeting,
a flint path from an old song,
the speech of flint and air,
flint and water, a ring with a horseshoe;
on the layered rock of the clouds
a milky sketch in slate—
not the schooldays of worlds
but the woolly visions of light sleep.

We sleep upright in the thick night
under the fleece hat.
The spring runs back whispering into the timbers
like a little chain, little warbler, speech.
Terror and Split write with the same little stick of milk.
Here, taking form, is the first draft
of the students of running water.

Steep goat cities.
The massive layering of flint.
And still the beds,
the sheep churches, the villages.
In the plumbline is their sermon,
in the water their lesson, time wears them fine,
and the transparent forest of the air
has been filled with them for a long time.

Like a dead hornet by the honey-comb
the pied day is swept out in disgrace.
The black night-harrier carries
burning chalk to feed the flint.
To erase day by day the writings
from the iconoclastic board,
and to shake visions, already transparent,
out of the hand like nestlings.

The fruit was coming to a head. The grapes ripening,
the day raging as a day rages.
Knucklebones—a gentle game—
and the coats of savage sheep-dogs, at noon.
Like rubble from icy heights,
from the backs of green icons,
the famished water flows, eddying,
playing like the young of an animal,

and crawls toward me like a spider,
over the moon-splashed crossings.
I hear the slate screech
on the startled crag.
Memory, are those your voices
teaching, splitting the night,
tossing slates into the forests,
ripping them from the beaks of birds?

Only the voice will teach us
what was clawing and fighting there.
And we will guide the callous slate
as the voice leads us.
I break the night, burning chalk
for the firm notation of a moment.
I exchange noise for the singing of arrows.
I exchange order for the fierce drumming of a grouse.

Who am I? No simple mason,
roofer or boatman.
I'm a double-dealer, with a double soul.
I'm the friend of night, the assassin of day.
Blessed is he who called the flint
the student of running water.
And blessed is he who buckled
the feet of the mountains onto solid ground.

Now I study the scratched diary
of the slate's summer,
the language of flint and air,
a layer of darkness, a layer of light.
I want to thrust my hand
into the flint path from an old song
as into a wound, and hold together
the flint and the water, the horseshoe and the ring.

1923

140

1 JANUARY 1924

Whoever kisses time's ancient nodding head
will remember later, like a loving son,
how the old man lay down to sleep
in the drift of wheat outside the window.
He who has opened the eyes of the age,
two large sleepy apples with inflamed lids,
hears forever after the roar of rivers
swollen with the wasted, lying times.

The age is a despot with two sleepy apples
to see with, and a splendid mouth of earth.
When he dies he'll sink onto the numb
arm of his son, who's already senile.
I know the breath growing weaker by the day.
Not long now till the simple song
of the wrongs of earth is cut off,
and a tin seal put on the lips.

O life of earth! O dying age!
I'm afraid no one will understand you
but the man with the helpless smile
of one who has lost himself.
O the pain of peeling back the raw eyelids
to look for a lost word, and with lime
slaking in the veins, to hunt
for night herbs for a tribe of strangers!

The age. In the sick son's blood the deposit of lime
is hardening. Moscow's sleeping like a wooden coffin.
There's no escaping the tyrant century.
After all these years the snow still smells of apples.
I want to run away from my own doorstep,
but where? Out in the street it's dark,
and my conscience glitters ahead of me
like salt strewn on the pavement.

Somehow I've got myself set for a short journey
through the back lanes, past thatched eaves, starling houses,
an everyday passer-by, in a flimsy coat,
forever trying to button the lap-robe.
Street after street flashes past,
the frozen runners crunch like apples;
can't get the button through the button-hole,
it keeps slipping out of my fingers.

The winter night thunders
like iron hardware through the Moscow streets.
Knocks like a frozen fish, or billows in steam,
flashing like a carp in a rosy tea-room.
Moscow is Moscow again. I say hello to her.
'Don't be stern with me; never mind.
I still respect the brotherhood
of the deep frost, and the pike's justice.'

The pharmacy's raspberry globe shines onto the snow.
Somewhere an Underwood typewriter's rattled.
The sleigh-driver's back, the snow knee-deep,
what more do you want? They won't touch you, won't kill you.
Beautiful winter, and the goat sky
has crumbled into stars and is burning with milk.
And the lap-robe flaps and rings
like horse-hair against the frozen runners.

And the lanes smoked like kerosene stoves,
swallowed snow, raspberry, ice,
endlessly peeling, like a Soviet sonatina,
recalling nineteen-twenty.
The frost is smelling of apples again.
Could I ever betray to gossip-mongers
the great vow to the Fourth Estate
and oaths solemn enough for tears?

Who else will you kill? Who else will you worship?
What other lie will you dream up?
There's the Underwood's cartilage. Hurry, rip out a key,
you'll find a little bone of a pike.
And in the sick son's blood the deposit of lime
will melt, and there'll be sudden blessèd laughter.
But the simple sonatina of typewriters
is only a faint shade of those great sonatas.   1924

Stanza 8, Fourth Estate: traditionally, the press (as an additional estate of the
realm, after the Lords Spiritual, the Lords Temporal, and the Commons).
Mandelstam's 'vow' should be read as a vow to spiritual and intellectual in-
dependence.

141

No, I was no one's contemporary—ever.
That would have been above my station.
How I loathe that other with my name.
He certainly never was me.

The age is a despot with two sleepy apples
to see with, and a splendid mouth of earth.
When he dies he'll subside onto the numb
arm of his son, who's already ageing.

As the age was born I opened my red eyelids,
my eyes were large sleepy apples.
The rivers thundered, informing me
of the bloodshot lawsuits of men.

A hundred years back,
on the camp-bed, on a drift of pillows,
there was a sprawled clay body: the age
getting over its first drunk.

What a frail bed, when you think
how the world creaks on its journey.
Well, we can't forge another.
We'd better get along with this one.

In stuffy rooms, in cabs, in tents,
the age is dying. Afterwards
flames will flutter like feathers, on the apple-skins,
on the curled wafers of horn.

Stanza 2: cf. previous poem. It is common in Mandelstam's practice for the
material of one poem to recur in slightly altered (and sometimes in identical)
form in an adjacent or related poem.

POEMS OF THE THIRTIES

201

Don't say a word to a soul.
Forget all you've seen,
bird, old woman, cage,
and the rest.

Or else at break of day
the moment you open your mouth,
you'll start to shiver
like the needles of a pine.

You'll see the wasp at the cottage,
pencil-case, ink stains,
blueberries ungathered
in those woods.

Tiflis. October 1930

202

Much we have to fear,
big-mouth beside me!

Our tobacco turns into dust,
nut-cracker, friend, idiot!

And I could have whistled through life like a starling,
eating nut pies . . . .

but clearly there's no chance of that.

Tiflis. October 1930

LENINGRAD

I've come back to my city. These are my own old tears,
my own little veins, the swollen glands of my childhood.

So you're back. Open wide. Swallow
the fish-oil from the river lamps of Leningrad.

Open your eyes. Do you know this December day,
the egg-yolk with the deadly tar beaten into it?

Petersburg! I don't want to die yet!
You know my telephone numbers.

Petersburg! I've still got the addresses:
I can look up dead voices.

I live on back stairs, and the bell,
torn out nerves and all, jangles in my temples.

And I wait till morning for guests that I love,
and rattle the door in its chains.

Leningrad. December 1930

222

I saw the world of power through a child's eyes—
oysters frightened me, I looked bashfully at the sentries—
I owe it not one jot of my soul:
something alien to me, which I never wanted.

I never stood under the bank's Egyptian porch,
stupidly pompous, in a beaver mitre, glowering.
Never, never, above the lemon Neva, to the rustle
of hundred rouble notes, did a gypsy girl dance for me.

Feeling executions on the way, I escaped from the roar
of rebellious events, to the Nereids on the Black Sea,
and from those days' beautiful women, gentle European women,
what anguish I consumed, what torment!

Why then does this city, even now, satisfy
my thoughts and my feelings at home in its ancient night?
It is more insolent than ever with its frost and fires,
more arrogant, damned, empty—it looks younger.

Maybe that's because, in a child's picture book,
I saw Lady Godiva draped in her red mane,
and I'm still whispering under my breath
Good-bye, Lady Godiva . . . Godiva, I've forgotten . . .

January 1931

Nereids: sea-nymphs, daughters of the ancient sea god Nereus.

223

O Lord, help me to live through this night—
I'm in terror for my life, your slave:
to live in Petersburg is to sleep in a grave.

January 1931

224

You and I will sit for a while in the kitchen,
the good smell of kerosene,

sharp knife, big round loaf—
Pump up the stove all the way.

And have some string handy
for the basket, before daylight,

to take to the station
where no one can come after us.

Leningrad. January 1931

After midnight the heart picks the locked silence
right out of your hands. Then it may remain
quiet, or it may raise the roof.
Like it or not, it's the only one of its kind.

Like it or not, you may know it but you'll never catch it,
so why shiver, now, like a thrown-out child?
After midnight the heart has its banquet,
gnawing on a silvery mouse.

Moscow. March 1931

227

For the sake of the future's trumpeting heroics,
for that exalted tribe,
I was robbed of my cup at my fathers' feast,
and of my laughter and honor.

The wolfhound age springs at my shoulders
though I'm no wolf by blood.
Better to be stuffed up a sleeve like a fleece cap
in a fur coat from the steppes of Siberia,

and so not see the snivelling, nor the sickly smears,
nor the bloody bones on the wheel,
so all night the blue foxes would still gleam
for me as they did in the first times.

Lead me into the night by the Yenesey
where the pine touches the star.
I'm no wolf by blood,
and only my own kind will kill me.

17–28 March 1931

My eyelashes are pins. In my chest one tear is boiling.
I'm not frightened to know that the storm will go on and on.
Some ghoul tries to hurry me, make me forget,
but even when I can't breathe I want to live till I die.

Hearing something, sitting up on the boards,
I look around wildly, still half asleep.
It's a prisoner intoning a rough song, at the hour
when dawn draws the first thread, outside the jail.

Moscow. March 1931

230

Outside the window, the darkness.
After me, the deluge.
Then what? The town snoring,
a mob in the cloak-room.

Masked ball. Wolfhound century.
Don't forget it.
Keep out of sight, a cap in a sleeve,
and God preserve you!

Moscow. March 1931

232

No, it's not for me to duck out of the mess
behind the cabdriver's back that's Moscow.
I'm the cherry swinging from the streetcar strap
of an evil time. What am I doing alive?

We'll take Streetcar A and then Streetcar B,
you and I, to see who dies first. As for Moscow,
one minute she's a crouched sparrow,
the next she's puffed up like a pastry—

how does she find time to threaten from holes?
You do as you please, I won't chance it.
My glove's not warm enough for the drive
around the whole whore Moscow.

April 1931

235

To Anna Akhmatova

Keep my words forever for their aftertaste of misfortune and
    smoke,
their tar of mutual tolerance, honest tar of work.
Sweet and black should be the water of Novgorod wells
to reflect the seven fins of the Christmas star.

And in return, father, friend, rough helper, I
the unrecognized brother, outlawed from the people's family,
promise to fit the beam-cages tight to the wells
so the Tartars can lower the princes in tubs, for torture.

O ancient headsman's blocks, keep on loving me!
Players in the garden seem to aim at death, and hit nine-pins.
I walk through my life aiming like that, in my iron shirt
(why not?) and I'll find an old beheading axe in the woods.

Khmelnitskaya. 3 May 1931

LAMARCK

There was an old man shy as a boy,
a gawky, timid patriarch—
who picked up the challenge for the honor of nature?
Who else? The man of passion, Lamarck.

If all that's alive is no more than a blot
for the brief escheated day,
give me the last rung
on Lamarck's moving ladder.

I'll hiss my way down through the lizards and snakes
to the annelid worms and the sea-slugs,
across resilient gangways, through valleys,
I'll shrink, and vanish, like Proteus.

I'll put on a shell cloak,
I'll be done with warm blood,
I'll grow suckers, I'll sink feelers
into the foam of the sea.

We went through the classes of insects
with their liquid liqueur-glass eyes.
He said, 'Nature's a shambles.
There's no vision. You're seeing for the last time.'

He said, 'No more harmony.
In vain you loved Mozart.
Now comes the deafness of spiders.
Here is ruin stronger than our strength.

Nature has gone away from us
as though she didn't need us.
She's slid the oblong brain
into a dark sheath, like a sword.

She's forgotten the drawbridge.
She lowered it late
for those with a green grave,
red breath, sinuous laughter . . .'   7–9 May 1932

BATYUSHKOV

An idler with a wand for a walking stick,
gentle Batyushkov lives with me,
strides down the alleys into Zamost'e,
sniffs a rose, sings Zafna—

nothing has ever been lost!
I believe I bowed when I met him,
and pressed his pale cold glove
like a man with a fever.

He smiled a little, I pronounced Thank you,
too shy to say any more.
No one else could trace those sounds,
no other waves sound the same.

He was bringing with him our anguish
and our great richness, and he was muttering:
the noise of making a poem, the bell of brotherhood,
the soft patter of tears,

still mourning for Tasso. And he answered me
'I can't get a taste for praise.
Only the grape-flesh of poetry
ever cooled my tongue.'

You that live in cities with city friends
would scarcely believe it:
eternal dreams, blood samples
pouring from one glass to the next.

Moscow. 18 June 1932

Konstantine Nikolaevich Batyushkov (1787–1855), a contemporary of Pushkin, was one of the greatest of Russian poets. 'The Dying Tasso' is among his best known poems. The name Zafna occurs in his poem 'Istochnik' (The Spring), 1810. Zamost'e is a town to the south-east of Lublin.

TO THE GERMAN LANGUAGE

Destroying myself, contradicting myself,
like the moth flying into the midnight flame,
suddenly all that binds me to our language
tempts me to leave it.

What is there between us? Praise without flattery.
Unfeigned friendship, face to face.
Let an alien family, to our west,
teach us seriousness and honor.

Poetry, you put storms to good use.
I remember a German officer,
his sword hilt wrapped with roses
and Ceres on his lips.

Already, in Frankfurt, the fathers were yawning,
and no one had yet heard of Goethe,
they were writing hymns, stallions were prancing
in their places, like letters of the alphabet.

Friends, tell me, in what Valhalla
did we crack nuts together, you and I?
What freedom was ours to spend as we pleased,
what landmarks did you leave for me?

And we ran straight from the first-rate newness
of a page of an almanac
down shallow steps, unafraid, into the grave,
as into a cellar to draw a jug of Moselle.

An alien language will be my swaddling clothes.
Long before I dared to be born
I was a letter of the alphabet, a verse like a vine,
I was the book that you all see in dreams.

When I was asleep and without feature
friendship woke me like a shot.
Nightingale-god, let Pylades' fate be mine,
or tear my tongue out, for it's no use to me.

Nightingale-god, I'm being conscripted still
for new plagues, for seven-year massacres.
Sound has shrivelled, words are hoarse and rebellious,
but you're alive still, and with you I'm at peace.

8–12 August 1932

267

ARIOSTO

Ariosto—no one in Italy more delightful—
these days has a frog in his throat.
He amuses himself with the names of fish,
he rains nonsense into the seas.

Like a musician with ten cymbals,
forever breaking in on his own music,
he leads us backwards and forwards, himself quite lost
in the maze of chivalric scandals.

A Pushkin in the language of the cicadas,
with a Mediterranean haughtiness to his melancholy,
he leaves his hero struggling with the preposterous,
and shudders, and is another man.

He says to the sea: roar but don't think!
To the maiden on the rock: lie there without bedclothes!
We've heard too little—tell us again,
while there's blood in the veins, and a roar in the ears.

O lizard city with a crust for a heart, and no soul,
Ferrara, give birth to more of such men!
While there's blood in the veins, hurry, tell the story
so often told, once more from the beginning.

It's cold in Europe. Italy is in darkness.
And power—it's like having to swallow a barber's hand.
But he goes on improving his act, playing
the great man smiling out of the window

at the lamb on the hill, the monk on his donkey,
the Duke's men-at-arms silly with wine
and the plague and garlic,
the baby dozing under a net of flies.

I love his desperate leisure,
his babble, the salt and sugar of his words,
the sounds happily conspiring in twos and threes.
Why should I want to split the pearl?

Ariosto, maybe this age will vanish
and we'll pour your azure and our Black Sea together
into one wide fraternal blue.
We too know it well. We've drunk mead on its shore.

Stary Krym. 4–6 May 1933

271

Cold spring, in starving Stary Krym,
still with its guilt, as it was under Wrangel.
Sheep-dogs in the courtyard, patches on the rags,
even the acrid smoke is the same.

And the empty distance as good as ever.
The trees with buds starting to swell
stand like shy strangers. The almond's pitiful,
decked out in yesterday's silliness.

Nature wouldn't know her own face.
From the Ukraine, the Kuban, terrible ghosts.
And the famished peasants, in felt shoes,
stand guard at their gates, never touching the rings.

Stary Krym. May 1933

Stary Krym: a small town in the Crimea, once its capital, where the Mandelstams
lived for a time during the terrible famine of 1932–33.

272

The apartment's dumb as paper,
it emptied by itself.
Sounds start slithering
through the radiator.

Our estate's in order:
telephone frozen into frog,
all our veteran possessions
homesick for the street.

A damnation of flimsy walls.
Nowhere to run to.
I'll have to play tunes on a comb
for somebody, like a clown.

Tunes ruder than students sing,
more insolent than young party members,
but I have to teach the hangmen,
perched on their school-bench, bird-notes.

I read ration-books.
I catch phrases like nooses.
I sing warning lullabies
to the rich peasant's good child.

Someone who draws from the life,
some fine-comb of the flax collective,
someone with blood in his ink
ought to sit on this stake.

Some respected informer, left
like salt when a purge boiled away,
some family's breadwinner
ought to crush this moth.

What teeth of malice lurking
in every detail,
as though Nekrasov's hammer
were still nailing the nails.

Let's start as though we were stretched
on the headsman's block, you and I,
on the other side of seventy years.
Old loafer, it's time for you to stamp your boots.

It won't be the fountain Hippocrene
that will burst through the hack-work walls,
but the current of household terror
in this evil coop in Moscow.

                    Moscow, Furmanov pereulok. November 1933

Stanza 8: Nikolay Alexeevich Nekrasov (1821–1878), the great realist and 'civic'
poet of the mid-nineteenth century.

286

[THE STALIN EPIGRAM]

Our lives no longer feel ground under them.
At ten paces you can't hear our words.

But whenever there's a snatch of talk
it turns to the Kremlin mountaineer,

the ten thick worms his fingers,
his words like measures of weight,

the huge laughing cockroaches on his top lip,
the glitter of his boot-rims.

Ringed with a scum of chicken-necked bosses
he toys with the tributes of half-men.

One whistles, another meouws, a third snivels.
He pokes out his finger and he alone goes boom.

He forges decrees in a line like horseshoes,
One for the groin, one the forehead, temple, eye.

He rolls the executions on his tongue like berries.
He wishes he could hug them like big friends from home.

[November 1933]

This poem, when word of it reached the authorities, was the occasion of Mandel-
stam's first arrest (1934). See Introduction.

287

As a stream falls from a single crack in a glacier
and its taste has two faces, one forward
one backward, and one is sweet and one hard,

so I die for the last time through each moment of these days,
and one way the old sighing frees me no longer,
and the other way the goal can no longer be seen.

Moscow. December 1933

To the memory of Andrey Bely

Blue eyes, and the bone of the forehead glowing—
the venom of the world that renews its youth was your guide.

And for the great magic that was to be yours
you were never to judge, never to curse.

They crowned you with a divine dunce-cap,
turquoise teacher, torturer, tyrant, fool.

A Gogol-ghost exploded like a blizzard in Moscow,
whirling, dense, clear, and unknowable.

With your collection of space and diploma of feathers,
author, young goldfinch, student, little student, sleighbell,

ice-skater, first-born, the age hauled you by the scruff
through new cases of words, still asleep under the snow.

Often one writes 'execution' and pronounces it 'song'.
Some ailments simplicity may have stung to death.

But our minds don't go off with a popgun straightness.
It's not the paper but the news that saves us.

As dragonflies, missing the water, land in the reeds,
so the fat pencils settled into the dead man,

sheets were unfolded on knees for our glorious future,
and they drew, apologizing to every line.

Between you and the country a link of ice is forming,
so lie there and grow young, and never melt

and let those to come, the young, let them never inquire
what it's like for you lying there, orphan, in the clean void.

Moscow. 10 January 1934

Andrey Bely (1880–1934), whose real name was Bugaev, was one of the greatest
of the Russian Symbolists. He was buried on 10 January 1934 (see following poem).

10 JANUARY 1934

I am haunted by a few chance phrases,
repeating all day 'the rich oil of my sadness'.
O God how black are the dragonflies of death,
how blue their eyes, and how black is that blue!

Where is the rule of the first-born? Or the felicity of custom?
Or the tiny hawk that melts deep in the eyes?
Or learning? Or the bitter taste of stealth?
Or the firm outline? Or the straightness of speech

honestly weaving back and forth,
a skater into a blue flame,
his blades in the frosty air braiding
the clink of glasses in a glacier?

Ahead of him solutions of three-layered salts,
the voices of German wise men,
fifty years of the glittering disputes
of the Russian first-born, rose in half an hour.

Suddenly music leapt from ambush—
a tiger was hiding in the instruments—
not to be heard, not to soften a thing,
it moved in the name of the muscles, of the drumming
          forehead,

of the tender mask just removed,
of the plaster fingers holding no pen,
of the puffed lips, of the hardened caress,
of the crystallized calm and goodness.

The furs on the coats breathed. Shoulder pressed shoulder.
Health was a red ore boiling—blood, sweat.
Sleep in the jacket of sleep, that held once
a dream of moving half a step forward.

And there was an engraver in the crowd
proposing to transfer onto pure copper
what the draftsmen, blackening paper,
merely sketched in split hair.

So I may hang on my own eyelashes,
swelling, ripening, reading all the parts in the play
till I'm picked.
The plot is the one thing we know.

January 1934

293

To Andrey Bely

The ranges of the Caucasus followed his baton,
he tramped the paths of the packed Alps, waving his arms;
looking around him, he rushed as though frightened
through the chatter of an endless crowd.

He brought across—as only one with the power could
      have done—
a crowd of minds, events, impressions:
Rachel looked into the mirror of phenomena,
and Leah wore a wreath as she sang.

Moscow. January 1934

295

Seamstress of bewitching glances,
heir to delicate shoulders,
at last the rough male has gone under—
speech is the drowned woman rising without words.

Fish move between blazing fins,
gills puffing water. Now
they're yours, pronouncing their soundless 'o's.
Feed them the bread of your body.

But we're not fish lapped in gold.
Our nurse was warm:
the flesh with its frail ribs,
the eyes' moist hollow fire.

Those poppy-stamens, your eyebrow, mark a dangerous race.
I'm in love like a Turkish soldier
with the defenceless crescent—your lip
and its small red wings.

Dear Turkish woman, never be angry.
I'll be sewn up in a sack with you,
for you I'll swallow your dark words,
I'll fill with the shapeless water.

Maria, help of the overwhelmed,
one can't wait for death, one must sleep.
I'm standing at your threshold. Please
go away. Please go. Please stay.

Moscow. February 1934

296

Your thin shoulders are for turning red under whips,
turning red under whips, and flaming in the raw cold.

Your child's fingers are for lifting flatirons,
for lifting flatirons, and for knotting cords.

Your tender soles are for walking on broken glass,
walking on broken glass, across bloody sand.

And I'm for burning like a black candle lit for you,
for burning like a black candle that dare not pray.

1934

Nereids, my Nereids,
sobbing is food and drink to you—
the daughters of the Mediterranean wrong
take offense at my compassion.

March [1935?]

299

BLACK EARTH

Manured, blackened, worked to a fine tilth, combed
like a stallion's mane, stroked under the wide air,
all the loosened ridges cast up in a single choir,
the damp crumbs of my earth and my freedom!

In the first days of plowing it's so black it looks blue.
Here the labor without tools begins.
A thousand mounds of rumor plowed open—I see
the limits of this have no limits.

Yet the earth's a mistake, the back of an axe;
fall at her feet, she won't notice.
She pricks up our ears with her rotting flute,
freezes them with the wood-winds of her morning.

How good the fat earth feels on the plowshare.
How still the steppe, turned up to April.
Salutations, black earth. Courage. Keep the eye wide.
Be the dark speech of silence laboring.

Voronezh. April 1935

'Black earth' (for the Russian *chernozem*) refers to the belt of rich black soil that
stretches from the Carpathians and the Black Sea to the Altay Mountains.

Earphones, earphones, who turned me in,
I won't let you forget these nights exiled on the steppe,
the lees of a voice on the radio at midnight resounding
from loudspeakers in Red Square.

How's the subway these days? Don't tell. Anything.
Don't ask how the buds are swelling.
You strokes of the Kremlin clock,
speech of the void shrunken to a point.

Voronezh. April 1935

l.1: the Russian *naushniki* means literally 'ear-phones' and, figuratively, 'informers', i.e. 'those who turn one in'.

303

—What street is this?
—Mandelstam Street.
—What the hell kind of name is that?
No matter which way you turn it
it comes out crooked.

—He wasn't a straight-edge exactly.
His morals resembled no lily.
And that's why this street (or rather,
to be honest, this sewer)
was given the name
of that Mandelstam.

Voronezh. April 1935

304

Now I lodge in the cabbage patches of the important.
A servant might come walking here out of an old song.
The factory winds work for nothing.
The road paved with brushwood runs into the distance.

At the edge of the steppe the plow has turned up night
bristling with a frost of tiny lights.
In the next room, in big boots,
the peeved landlord stomps and stomps

over the floor, the deck, the coffin-lids
warped into crusts.
Not much sleep under strange roofs
with my life far away.

Voronezh. April 1935

305

I have to live, even though I died twice
and the town went half mad on water.

How handsome it looks, how high in heart and cheekbone,
how good the fat slice of earth on the plowshare.

How still the steppe, turned over in April.
But the sky, the sky—your Michelangelo!   [1935]

306

Now I'm dead in the grave with my lips moving
and every schoolboy repeating the words by heart.

The earth is rounder in Red Square than anywhere,
all one side of a hardened will.

The earth in Red Square is rounder than anywhere.
No one would think it was so light of heart

bending back all the way down to the rice growing
on the last day of the last slave on the globe.

Voronezh. May 1935

307

You took away all the oceans and all the room.
You gave me my shoe-size in earth with bars around it.
Where did it get you? Nowhere.
You left me my lips, and they shape words, even in silence.

Voronezh [1935]

308

How dark it gets along the Kama.
The cities kneel by the river on oaken knees.

Draped in cobwebs, beard with beard,
black firs and their reflections run back into their childhood.

The water leaned into fifty-two pairs of oars,
pushed them upstream, downstream, to Kazan and Cherdyn.

There I floated with a curtain across the window,
a curtain across the window, and the flame inside was my head.

And my wife was with me there five nights without sleeping,
five nights awake keeping an eye on the guards.

Voronezh. May 1935

After his first arrest, Mandelstam was exiled to the town of Cherdyn in the Urals.
With his wife by his side he made part of the journey there along the river Kama.

I left with the evergreen east in my eyes.
The Kama and its riches dragged at the buoy.

Let me cut the hill and its campfire into layers.
There'll be no time to grow forests.

Let me settle here, right here.
Some people live here. The Urals live on and on.

Let me take this mirror country lying on its back
and button a long coat over it and keep it warm.

Voronezh. May 1935

312

STANZAS

1 I don't want to pay down the last penny of my soul
  among hothouse adolescents. I go to the world
  as the single peasant goes to the collective
  and I find the people good.

2 I'm for the Red Army style overcoat,
  down to the heels, simple flat sleeves,
  cut like a rain cloud over the Volga,
  to hang full on the chest, one fold down the back,
  no stuff wasted on double hems;
  you can roll it up in the summer.

3 A damned seam, a foolishness,
  came between us. Now let it be clear:
  I have to live, breathing and bolshevescent.
  I'll be better-looking before I die,
  staying to play among the people.

4 When you think how I raced around
in a seven-inch sweat, in dear old Cherdyn,
among the bell-bottomed river smells,
not stopping to watch the goat-squabbles—
a rooster in the transparent summer night.
Grub and spit, and something, and babble—and got
the woodpecker off my back. One jump—then sane again.

5 And you my sister Moscow, how light you are,
coming to meet your brother's plane
before the first street-car bell.
You are gentler than the sea, you tossed salad
of wood, glass, milk.

6 Once my country talked with me,
indulged me, scolded me a little, never read me.
But when I grew up and was a witness
she noticed me all at once, and like a lens
set me alight with one flash from the Admiralty.

7 I have to live, breathing and bolshevescent,
laboring with language, disobeying, I and one other.
I hear the Arctic throbbing with Soviet pistons.
I remember everything—the necks of German brothers,
the gardener-executioner whose pastime
was the Lorelei's lilac comb.

8 I'm not robbed blind, not desperate,
just, only, merely, thrown.
When my string's tuned tight as Igor's Song,
when I get my breath back, you can hear
in my voice the earth, my last weapon,
the dry dampness of acres of black earth.

Voronezh. May–June 1935

Stanza 6: the Admiralty is one of the most notable buildings and the central focal
point of St. Petersburg (Leningrad).
Stanza 8: the Song of Igor is the principal monument of early Russian Literature.

'No, it's not migraine, but hand me the menthol pencil—
neither art's languid invitation, nor the fireworks of space.'

Life began in a trough, with a damp lisping whisper,
and went on into the soft soot of kerosene.

Then at some dacha, in a green shagreen binding,
it suddenly blazed up in lilac flames, no one knew why.

'No, it's not migraine, but hand me the menthol pencil—
neither art's languid invitation, nor the fireworks of space.'

Later, with straining eyes, through stained glass, painfully,
I see the sky, a club threatening, and the earth, a red bald spot.

After that I forget. It seems to break off
With a faint smell of resin, and what must be rotten whale oil.

No, not migraine, but the cold of neuter space,
the sharp sound of gauze tearing, the rumble of the carbolic
    guitar.   Voronezh. 23 April–July 1935

320

I want to give back this dust I've borrowed,
not as the flour from a white butterfly;
I want this thinking body
this vertebrate, this burnt body
that once knew its length, to be changed
into a thoroughfare, a country.

The dark pine needles shout.
The wreaths deep as wells,

the hoops of red-flagged needles
leaning on the lathes of death,
'o''s from an alphabet,
prolong a time once loved, a life.

The latest recruits were carrying out
orders under the hardened sky.
Infantry passed, under their rifles—
so many silent exclamations.

Blue eyes, hazel eyes,
guns aimed at the air in thousands,
in confusion—men, men, men—
who will come after them?

Voronezh. 21 July 1935

324

My goldfinch, I'll cock my head;
together we'll look at the world:
the winter day jagged as stubble,
is it rough to your eye as to mine?

Tail, little black and yellow boat.
Head dipped in color past the beak.
Goldfinch, do you know you're a goldfinch,
do you know how much?

What's the atmosphere back of his forehead?
It's black, red, yellow, white.
He keeps an eye out both ways. Now he's stopped
looking—he's flown from between them!

Voronezh. December 1936

It's not I, it's not you—it's they
who've locked up all the word endings.
The air that makes flutes of the reeds is theirs.
Human lips are snails, happy
to be laden with their breathing.

They have no names. He who enters their cartilage
falls heir to their domains.

And to men, their living hearts,
wandering the split paths, turning,
the pleasures you tell of will all be theirs,
and the pain that drives them back and forth in tides.

Voronezh. 9–27 December 1936

329

Today is all beak and no feathers
and it's staying that way. Why?
And a gate by the sea gazes at me
out of anchors and fogs.

Quietly, quietly warships are gliding
through faded water,
and in canals gaunt as pencils
under the ice the leads go on blackening.

Voronezh. 9–28 December 1936

The idol is motionless inside the hill,
an endless serenity in the ordered rooms.
Drops of oil strung round his neck
watch over the tides of sleep.

When he was a boy with a tame peacock
they gave him a rainbow to eat
and milk in clay roses
and they surrounded him with scarlet.

Now every bone is tied in a trance.
The knees are a man's, the shoulders and arms are a man's.
The whole of his mouth is a smile.
Thinking bone by bone, feeling with his forehead,
laboriously he resurrects what it was to be human.

Voronezh. December 1936

341

Mounds of human heads are wandering into the distance.
I dwindle among them. Nobody sees me. But in books
much loved, and in children's games I shall rise
from the dead to say the sun is shining.   [1936–1937?]

343

Dead poet with a ring for a name,
I'm near you, and I'm ringed too, like a falcon.
No messenger comes for me.
There's no step up to my door.

There's a forest of pines, of ink,
chained to my leg.
The horizon lies open, messenger
of no message.

The little mounds straggle on the steppe—
nomads. And the camps of the nights
keep moving on, the little nights
keep moving, leading their blind men.

Voronezh. 1–9 January 1937

344

When the sorcerer sets
the colors of horses
to whispering
in the sagging boughs,

the faded lazy hero,
bullfinch in winter,
small but strong,
is not in the mood for song.

The sky will lean out and over.
Under its raised brows I'll hurry
to my seat
in the lilac sleigh of the dead.

Voronezh. 6–10 January 1937

From what bleeding veins of ore
will the dear yeast of the world return to me
the accents, tears, labors,
the seething murmur of trouble,
all the lost sounds?

In my beggar's mind, for the first time,
ditches open, full of brassy water,
and I follow them away from myself,
loathing each step, unknown to myself,
both the blind man and his guide.

Voronezh. 12–18 January 1937

A little imp in wet fur
has crawled—well, where could he go—
into the thimbles under the hooves,
into the rushing tracks.
Kopeck by kopeck the seven-league air
picks the village bare.

The road splashes in the mirrors.
The rushing tracks
will stay there a while
with no shroud or mica.
The wheel beats at an angle.
Given up. Things could be worse.

I'm bored. My true work
babbles away, off the track.
Some other's come from the side,
and mocked, and knocked the axle crooked.

Voronezh. 12–18 January 1937

349

I am alone staring into the eye of the ice.
He is going nowhere. I came from there.
A miracle: the plain ironed to the end
of time, pleated without a wrinkle, is breathing.

The sun squints, a starched pauper;
calm grimace, source of calm.
The forests stretch to ten figures, almost complete.
The eyes bite on virgin bread, on snow.

Voronezh. 16 January 1937

350

What can we do with the plains' beaten weight?
No one can believe the slow hunger in them.
We think it's theirs, the vast flatness, but on the journey
to sleep, there it is in ourselves, there it is.

Farther and farther the question spreads—where are they going
and coming from? And crawling across them
is that not the one whose name we shriek in our sleep—
the Judas of nations unborn?

Voronezh. 16 January 1937

351

Oh the horizon steals my breath and takes it nowhere—
I'm choked with space!
I get my breath back, there's the horizon again.
I want something to cover my eyes.

I'd have liked the sand better—a life in layers
along the sawing shores of the river.
I'd have clung to the sleeves of the shy current,
to eddies, hollows, shallows.

We'd have worked well together, for a moment,
a century. I've wanted rapids like those.
I'd have laid my ear under the bark of drifting logs
to hear the rings marching outward.

Voronezh. 16 January 1937

353

What has held out against oxidation
and adulteration, burns like feminine silver,
and quiet labor silvers the iron plow
and the poet's voice.   Voronezh. [1937]

354a

You're still alive, you're not alone yet—
she's still beside you, with her empty hands,
and a joy reaches you both across immense plains
through mists and hunger and flying snow.

Opulent poverty, regal indigence!
Live in it calmly, be at peace.
Blessed are these days, these nights,
and innocent is the labor's singing sweetness.

Miserable is the man who runs from a dog
in his shadow, whom a wind reaps at the knees,
and poor the one who holds out his rag of life
to beg mercy of a shadow.

Voronezh. January 1937

Now I'm in the spider-web of light.
The people with all the shadows of their hair
need light and the pale blue air
and bread, and snow from the peak of Elbrus.

And there's no one I can ask about it.
Alone, where would I look?
These clear stones weeping themselves
come from no mountains of ours.

The people need poetry that will be their own secret
to keep them awake forever,
and bathe them in the bright-haired wave
of its breathing.

Voronezh. 19 January 1937

Stanza 1: Elbrus is the highest mountain in the main range of the Caucasus.

357

Once a line of verse, in disgrace, father unknown,
fell from the sky like a stone, waking the earth somewhere.
No supplication can alter the poet's invention.
It can only be what it is. No one will judge it.

Voronezh. 20 January 1937

358

I hear, I hear the first ice
rustling under the bridges,
and I think of drunkenness swimming
radiant above our heads.

From stagnant stairs, from squares
flanked with jagged palaces
Dante's exhausted lips
more resonantly sang
his circling Florence.

So my shade with its eyes
gnaws the grains of that granite
and at night sees a hill of logs
that by day had seemed to be houses.

My shade twirls its thumbs, or yawns,
when there's no one but us,

or it kicks up a din, in company,
warmed by their wine and their sky,

and flings sour bread
to the importunate swans.

Voronezh. 21–22 January 1937

360

What shall I do with myself, now it's January?
The gaping city staggers and clings.
I think it's the locked doors that have made me drunk.
I could howl out of every lock and paper-clip.

The stocking-lanes barking,
knitted streets of junk-rooms,
idiots ducking into corners
to jump out of them—

in the pit, in the warty darkness,
I'm slipping toward the frozen pump-house.
I fall over my feet. I swallow dead air.
A fever of crows explodes.

And after that, there I am, gasping,
drumming on an icy wooden tub:
'Somebody read me! Somebody lead me! Somebody heal me!
Somebody say something on the jagged stairs!'

Voronezh. January–February 1937

364

I've gone, like the martyr of light and shade,
like Rembrandt, into a growing numbness of time.
One of my ribs is a burning blade,
but it's not in the keeping of these watchmen
nor of this soldier asleep under the storm.

Sir, magnificent brother, master
of the black-green darkness, may you forgive me:
the eye of the falcon-quill pen
and the hot casks in the midnight harem
waken, but waken to no good
the tribe frightened by furs in the twilight.

Voronezh. 8 February 1937

365

I sing from a wet throat and a dry soul,
vision properly moist, a mind behaving itself.
Is wine good for a man? Are furs
and the blood heaving with all that is Colchis?
But something is clenched in my chest. There's a hush there.
                                        No language.
It's no longer me singing, it's my breath.
And my hearing's sheathed in a mountain. My head is deaf.

A selfless song is its own praise.
A comfort for friends, and for enemies, pitch.

A selfless song growing out of moss,
the one-voiced gift from the hunter's life,
which they sing riding the heights on horses,
with breath honest and open,
in honor and sternness caring only
to bring the young pair sinless to their wedding.

Voronezh. 8 February 1937

366

Sunderings of round bays, the gravel, the blue,
and the slow sail turning at last into a cloud—
almost before I prized you I was taken from you.
Longer than organ fugues, and bitter, is the sea grass,
pretending to be hair, and smelling of the long lie.
My head is awash with an iron tenderness.
Rust is nibbling along the gradual shore. . . .
Why was this different sand put under my head?

O guttural Urals, broad-shouldered lands of the Volga,
wide plains facing me—all my rights are there,
and I must still fill my lungs with them.

Voronezh. 8 February 1937

367

Armed with the sight of the fine wasps
sucking at the earth's axis, the earth's axis,
I recall each thing that I've had to meet,
I remember it by heart, and in vain.

I do not draw or sing
or ply the dark-voiced bow.
I make a little hole in life. How I envy
the strength and cunning of the wasps!

Oh if only once the sting of the air and the heat
of summer could make me hear
beyond sleep and death
the earth's axis, the earth's axis.

Voronezh. 8 February 1937

375

On a board of raspberry and pure gold,
on the side of Deep Saddle-Bow Mountain,
monstrous under drifted snow,
the sleigh-tracked, sleepy, horse-drawn
half town half river-bank, hitched up
in a harness of red coals, heated
with yellow resin burnt down to a sugar-tar,
was carried away.

Do not hunt here for the heaven of burnt oils
or the ice-skating Flemish brush-stroke.

There's no merry, gnarled, gnomish flock
in ear-flapped caps cawing here.

And do not trouble me with comparison,
but cut off my drawing that's in love with the long road,
like the maple bough, dry but still living,
which the smoke, running on stilts, carries away.

Voronezh. 6 March 1937

THE LAST SUPPER

The heaven of the supper fell in love with the wall.
It filled it with cracks. It fills them with light.
It fell into the wall. It shines out there
in the form of thirteen heads.

And that's my night sky, before me,
and I'm the child standing under it,
my back getting cold, an ache in my eyes,
and the wall-battering heaven battering me.

At every blow of the battering ram
stars without eyes rain down,
new wounds in the last supper,
the unfinished mist on the wall.

Voronezh. 9 March 1937

378

I've lost my way in the sky—now where?
Let the one with the sky nearest to him answer.
It was easier for Dante's nine fallen
discuses to ring.

You can't cut me off from life—it dreams
of killing and caressing at a turn of the same hand,
so an anguish from Florence still
fills the ears, the eyes, the sockets.

No, do not oppress my forehead
with the sharp green laurel.
Better to cleave my heart
into blue shards, ringing,

then when I die, keeping faith
to the last with the lovers,
every sky in my breast will echo,
ringing out, and up.

Voronezh. 9–19 March 1937

380

Maybe this is the beginning of madness.
Maybe it's your conscience:
a knot of life in which we are seized and known
and untied for existence.

So in cathedrals of crystals not found on earth
the prudent spider of light
draws the ribs apart and gathers them again
into one bundle.

And gathered together by one thin beam
the bundles of pure lines give thanks.
One day they will meet, they will assemble
like guests with the visors up,

and here on earth, not in heaven,
as in a house filled with music,
if only we don't offend them, or frighten them away.
How good to live to see it!

Forgive me for what I am saying.
Read it to me quietly, quietly.

Voronezh. 15 March 1937

WINEJUG

Bad debtor to an endless thirst,
wise pander of wine and water,
the young goats jump up around you
and the fruits are swelling to music.

The flutes shrill, they rail and shriek
because the black and red all around you
tell of ruin to come
and no one there to change it.

Voronezh. 21 March 1937

384

How I wish I could fly
where no one could see me,
behind the ray of light
leaving no trace.

But you—let the light encircle you.
That's the one happiness.
Learn from a star the meaning
of light.

If it's a ray, if it's light,
that's only because
the whisper and chatter of lovers
strengthen and warm it.

And I want to tell you
that I'm whispering,
I'm giving you to the ray,
little one, in whispers.

Voronezh. 23 March 1937

Just for its potters the dark blue island,
Crete, the lighthearted, is great. When the earth they baked
rings you can hear their genius.
Do you hear fins of dolphins beating deep in the earth?

Speak of this sea and it will rise
in the clay, to smile in its oven.
and the frigid power of the vessel
became half sea, half eye.

Blue island, give me back what is mine.
Flying Crete, give back my work to me.
Fill the baked vessel
from the breasts of the flowing goddess.

This was, and was sung, and turned blue
in days before Odysseus,
before food and drink
were called 'my,' 'mine'.

Grow strong again and shine
o star of ox-eyed heaven,
and you, flying-fish of chance,
and you, o water saying yes.

Voronezh. March [1937]

387

As though the fame of its mint and iota
were never enough, the Greek flute,
free, following its instincts,
matured, labored, crossed ditches.

No one can escape it,
nor quiet it, through clenched teeth,
nor coax it into speech with the tongue,
nor shape it with the lips.

And peace will never come to the flutist.
He feels that he is alone.
He remembers moulding his native sea
out of lilac clays, long ago.

With a sonorous climbing whisper,
with the patter of lips remembering,
he hurries to be thrifty,
he selects sounds, a neat miser.

When he's gone, we'll have no one
to knead lumps of clay to death.
When the sea filled me
my measure sickened me.

And in my own lips there's no peace.
'Mouther''s too close to 'murder'.
I let the flute's equinox
drop lower and lower.

Voronezh. 7 April 1937

388

I raise this green to my lips,
this muddy promise of leaves,
this forsworn earth,
mother of snowdrops and of every tree.

See how I'm blinded but strengthened,
surrendering to the least of the roots?
Are my eyes not blown out
by the exploding trees?

The little frogs are rolled up in their voices,
drops of mercury, huddled in a ball.
The twigs are turning into branches, and the fallow ground
is a mirage of milk.

Voronezh. 30 April 1937

393

Pear blossom and cherry blossom aim at me.
Their strength is crumbling but they never miss.

Stars in clusters of blossoms, leaves with stars—
what twin power is there? On what branch does truth blossom?

It fires into the air with flower or strength.
Its air-white full blossom-bludgeons put it to death.

And the twin scent's sweetness is unwelcoming.
It contends, it reaches out, it is mingled, it is sudden.

Voronezh. 4 May 1937

394

Limping like a clock on her left leg,
at the beloved gait, over the empty earth,
she keeps a little ahead of the quick girl,
her friend, and the young man almost her age.
What's holding her back
drives her on.
What she must know is coming
drags at her foot. She must know
that under the air, this spring,
our mother earth is ready for us
and that it will go on like this forever.

There are women with the dampness of the earth in their veins.
Every step they take there's a sobbing in a vault.
They were born to escort the dead, and be at the grave
first to greet those who rise again.
It would be terrible to want a caress from them
but to part with them is more than a man could do.
One day angel, next day the worm in the grave,
the day after that, a sketch.
What used to be within reach—out of reach.
Flowers never die. Heaven is whole.
But ahead of us we've only somebody's word.

Voronezh. 4 May 1937

395

Through Kiev, through the streets of the monster
some wife's trying to find her husband.
One time we knew that wife,
the wax cheeks, dry eyes.

Gypsies won't tell fortunes for beauties.
Here the concert hall has forgotten the instruments.
Dead horses along the main street.
The morgue smells in the nice part of town.

The Red Army trundled its wounded
out of town on the last street car,
one blood-stained overcoat calling,
'Don't worry, we'll be back!'

Voronezh. May 1937

CONVERSATION ABOUT DANTE

Translated by Clarence Brown & Robert Hughes
circa 1934–35

Così gridai colla faccia levata.[1]*
(*Inferno,* XVI, 76)

I.

Poetic speech is a crossbred process, and it consists of two
sonorities. The first of these is the change that we hear and
sense in the very instruments of poetic speech, which arise in
the process of its impulse. The second sonority is the speech
proper, that is, the intonational and phonetic work performed
by the said instruments.

Understood thus, poetry is not a part of nature, not even
the best or choicest part. Still less is it a reflection of nature,
which would lead to a mockery of the law of identity; but it is
something that, with astonishing independence, settles down
in a new extraspatial field of action, not so much narrating
nature as acting it out by means of its instruments, which are
commonly called images.

It is only very conditionally possible to speak of poetic
speech or thought as sonorous, for we hear in it only the cross-
ing of two lines, and of these one, taken by itself, is absolutely

*"Conversation about Dante" includes several passages from the *Commedia* that
Mandelstam himself translated, often quite freely. Here these have been translated
from the Russian, with the original Italian and a literal English rendering appearing
in the notes. Literal translations of passages and lines from Dante that Mandelstam
quotes in Italian can also be found in the notes. The source for the English transla-
tions is the Temple Classics edition of the *Commedia*, sometimes slightly modified.

mute, while the other, taken apart from its instrumental metamorphosis, is devoid of all significance and all interest and is subject to paraphrase, which is in my opinion the truest sign of the absence of poetry. For where one finds commensurability with paraphrase, there the sheets have not been rumpled; there poetry has not, so to speak, spent the night.

Dante is a master of the instruments of poetry and not a manufacturer of images. He is a strategist of transformations and crossbreedings, and least of all is he a poet in the "All-European" and outwardly cultural sense of this word.

The wrestlers winding themselves into a tangle in the arena may be regarded as an example of a transformation of instruments and a harmony.

These naked and glistening wrestlers who walk about pluming themselves on their physical prowess before grappling in the decisive fight. . . .[2]

The modern cinema, meanwhile, with its metamorphosis of the tapeworm, turns into a malicious parody on the function of instruments in poetic speech, since its frames move without any conflict and merely succeed one another.

Imagine something understood, grasped, torn out of obscurity, in a language voluntarily and willingly forgotten immediately upon the completion of the act of understanding and execution.

In poetry only the executory understanding has any importance, and not the passive, the reproducing, the paraphrasing understanding. Semantic satisfaction is equivalent to the feeling of having carried out a command.

The wave signals of meaning disappear once they have done their work: the more powerful they are, the more yielding, and the less prone to linger.

Otherwise one cannot escape the rote drilling, the hammering in of those prepared nails called "cultural-poetic" images.

External, explanatory imagery is incompatible with the presence of instruments.

The quality of poetry is determined by the rapidity and decisiveness with which it instills its command, its plan of action, into the instrumentless, dictionary, purely qualitative nature of word formation. One has to run across the whole width of the river, jammed with mobile Chinese junks sailing in various directions. This is how the meaning of poetic speech is created. Its route cannot be reconstructed by interrogating the boatmen: they will not tell how and why we were leaping from junk to junk.

Poetic speech is a carpet fabric with a multitude of textile warps which differ one from the other only in the coloring of the performance, only in the musical score of the constantly changing directives of the instrumental code of signals.

It is a most durable carpet, woven out of water: a carpet in which the currents of the Ganges (taken as a textile theme) do not mix with the samples of the Nile and the Euphrates, but remain many-hued, in braids, figures, and ornaments—but not in regular patterns, for a pattern is that very paraphrase of which we were speaking. Ornament is good by virtue of the fact that it preserves the traces of its origin as a performed piece of nature—animal, vegetable, steppe, Scythian, Egyptian, what you will, national or barbarian, it is always speaking, seeing, active.

Ornament is stanzaic.

Pattern is a matter of lines.

The poetic hunger of the old Italians is magnificent, their animal, youthful appetite for harmony, their sensual lust after rhyme—*il disio.*

The mouth works, the smile moves the verse line, the lips are cleverly and merrily crimson, the tongue presses itself trustfully to the roof of the mouth.

The inner image of the verse is inseparable from the numberless changes of expression which flit across the face of the teller of tales as he talks excitedly.

For that is exactly what the act of speech does: it distorts our face, explodes its calm, destroys its mask.

When I began to study Italian and had only just become slightly acquainted with its phonetics and prosody, I suddenly understood that the center of gravity of the speech movements had been shifted closer to the lips, to the external mouth. The tip of the tongue suddenly acquired a place of honor. The sound rushed toward the canal lock of the teeth. Another observation that struck me was the infantile quality of Italian phonetics, its beautiful childlike quality, its closeness to infant babbling, a sort of immemorial Dadaism:

> e consolando usava l'idioma
> che pria li padri e le madri trastulla
>
> .   .   .   .
>
> favoleggiava con la sua famiglia
> dei Troiani, di Fiesole e di Roma.[3]
> (*Paradiso*, XV, 122–123, 125–126)

Would you like to become acquainted with the lexicon of Italian rhymes? Take the entire Italian dictionary and leaf through as you please. Here everything rhymes. Every word cries out to enter into *concordanza*.

There is a marvelous abundance of endings that are wed to each other. The Italian verb gains force as it approaches its end and only in the ending does it live. Every word hastens to burst forth, to fly from the lips, go away, and clear a place for the others.

When it became necessary to trace the circumference of a time for which a millennium was less than the wink of an eyelash, Dante introduced an infantile "transsense"[4] language into his astronomical, *concertante*, deeply public, pulpit lexicon.

The creation of Dante is above all the emergence into the world arena of the Italian language of his day, its emergence as a whole, as a system.

The most Dadaist of all the Romance languages moved into first place internationally.

II.

It is essential to demonstrate some bits and pieces of Dante's rhythms. This is an unexplored area, but one that must become known. Whoever says, "Dante is sculptural," is enslaved by beggarly definitions of a magnificent European. Dante's poetry is characterized by all the forms of energy known to modern science. Unity of light, sound, and matter constitutes its inner nature. The labor of reading Dante is above all endless, and the more we succeed at it the farther we are from our goal. If the first reading results only in shortness of breath and wholesome fatigue, then equip yourself for subsequent readings with a pair of indestructible Swiss boots with hobnails. The question occurs to me—and quite seriously—how many sandals did Alighieri wear out in the course of his poetic work, wandering about on the goat paths of Italy?

The *Inferno* and especially the *Purgatorio* glorify the human gait, the measure and rhythm of walking, the foot and its shape.

The step, linked to the breathing and saturated with thought: this Dante understands as the beginning of prosody. In order to indicate walking he uses a multitude of varied and charming turns of phrase.

In Dante philosophy and poetry are forever on the move, forever on their feet. Even standing still is a variety of accumulated motion; making a space for people to stand and talk takes as much trouble as scaling an alp. The metrical foot of his poetry is the inhalation; the exhalation is the step. The step draws a conclusion, invigorates, syllogizes.

A good education is a school of the most rapid associations: you grasp things on the wing, you are sensitive to allusions—this is Dante's favorite form of praise.

As Dante understands it, the teacher is younger than the pupil, because he "runs faster."

> He [Brunetto Latini] turned aside and seemed to me like one of those who run races through the green meadows in the environs of Verona, and his whole bearing bespoke his belonging to the number of winners, not the vanquished.[5]
>
> (*Inferno*, XV, 121–124)

The rejuvenating force of metaphor returns to us the educated old man Brunetto Latini in the guise of a youthful victor in a track race in Verona.

What is Dantean erudition?

Aristotle, like a downy butterfly, is fringed with the Arabian border of Averroës.

> Averrois che il gran comento feo[6]
> (*Inferno*, IV, 144)

In the present case the Arab Averroës accompanies the Greek Aristotle. They are the components of the same drawing. There is room for them on the membrane of one wing.

The end of Canto IV of the *Inferno* is a genuine orgy of quotations. I find here a pure and unalloyed demonstration of Dante's keyboard of allusions.

It is a keyboard promenade around the entire mental horizon of antiquity. A kind of Chopin polonaise in which an armed Caesar with the blood-red eyes of a griffin appears alongside Democritus, who took matter apart into atoms.

A quotation is not an excerpt. A quotation is a cicada. It is part of its nature never to quiet down. Once having got hold of the air, it does not release it. Erudition is far from being the same thing as the keyboard of allusions, which is the main essence of an education.

I mean to say that a composition is formed not from a heaping up of particulars but in consequence of the fact that one detail after another is torn away from the object, leaves it, flutters out, is hacked away from the system, and goes off into its own functional space or dimension, but each time at a strictly specified moment and provided the general situation is sufficiently mature and unique.

Things themselves we do not know; on the other hand, we are highly sensitive to their location. And so, when we read the cantos of Dante, we receive as it were communiqués from a military field of operations and from them we can very well surmise how the sounds of the symphony of war are struggling with each other, even though each bulletin taken separately brings the news of some slight shift here or there of the flags showing strategic positions or indicates some change or other in the timbre of the cannonade.

Thus, the thing arises as an integral whole as a result of the one differentiating impulse which runs all through it. It does not continue looking like itself for the space of a single minute. If a physicist should conceive the desire, after taking apart the nucleus of an atom, to put it back together again, he would be like the partisans of descriptive and explanatory poetry, for whom Dante represents, for all time, a plague and a threat.

If we were to learn to hear Dante, we should hear the ripening of the clarinet and the trombone, we should hear the viola transformed into the violin and the lengthening of the valve of the French horn. And we should see forming around the lute and the theorbo the hazy nucleus of the homophonic three-part orchestra of the future.

Further, if we were to hear Dante, we should be unexpectedly plunged into a power flow which is sometimes, as a whole, called "composition," sometimes, in particular, "metaphor," and sometimes, because of its evasive quality, "simile," and which gives birth to attributes in order that they might return into it, increase it by their melting and, having scarcely achieved the first joy of coming into existence, immediately lose their primogeniture in attaching themselves to the matter that is straining in among the thoughts and washing against them.

The beginning of Canto X of the *Inferno*. Dante shoves us into the inner blindness of the compositional clot: "We now entered upon a narrow path between the wall of the cliff and those in torment—my teacher and I at his back." Every effort is directed toward the struggle against the density and gloom of the place. Lighted shapes break through like teeth. Conversation is as necessary here as torches in a cave.

Dante never enters upon single-handed combat with his material unless he has prepared an organ with which to apprehend it, unless he has equipped himself with some measuring instrument for calculating concrete time, dripping or melting. In poetry, where everything is measure and everything proceeds out of measure and turns around it and for its sake, measuring instruments are tools of a special quality, performing a special, active function. Here the trembling hand of the compass not only humors the magnetic storm, but produces it.

And thus we see that the dialogue of Canto X of the *Inferno* is magnetized by the tense forms of the verbs. The past imperfect and perfect, the past subjunctive, the present itself and the future are, in the tenth canto, given categorically, authoritatively.

The entire canto is built on several verbal thrusts, which leap boldly out of the text. Here the table of conjunctions has an air of fencing about it, and we literally hear how the verbs kill time. First lunge:

> La gente, che per li sepolcri giace,
>> *potrebbesi* veder? . . .
>>> (*Inferno*, X, 7–8)

> These people, laid in open graves,
>> may I be permitted to see?[7]

Second lunge: "Volgiti: che fai?" [line 31]. This contains the horror of the present tense, a kind of *terror praesentis*.

Here the unalloyed present is taken as a charm to ward off evil. In complete isolation from the future and the past, the present tense is conjugated like pure fear, like danger.

Three nuances of the past tense, washing its hands of any responsibility for what has already taken place, are given in this tercet:

> I [had] fixed my gaze upon him
>> And he drew himself up to his full height
>> As though [he were] insulting Hell with his immense disdain.[8]

(Inferno, X, 34–36)

And then, like a powerful tube, the past breaks upon us in the question of Farinata: "Who were your ancestors?" (*Chi fur li maggior tui?*) [line 42]. How the copula, the little truncated form *fur* instead of *furon*, is stretched out here! Was this not the manner in which the French horn was formed, by lengthening the valve?

Later there is a slip of the tongue in the form of the past definite. This slip of the tongue was the final blow to the elder Cavalcanti: he heard Alighieri, one of the contemporaries and comrades of his son, Guido Cavalcanti, the poet, still living at the time, say something—it does not matter what—with the fatal past definite form *ebbe*.

And how remarkable that it is precisely this slip which opens the way for the main stream of the dialogue. Cavalcanti fades out like an oboe or clarinet that had played its part, and Farinata, like a deliberate chess player, continues the interrupted move and renews the attack:

> "E sè," continuando al primo detto,
>> "s'egli han quell'arte," disse "male appresa,
>> ciò mi tormenta più che questo letto."[9]

(Inferno, X, 76–78)

The dialogue in the tenth canto of the *Inferno* is an unexpected clarifier of the situation. It flows all by itself from the space between the two rivers of speech.

All useful information of an encyclopedic nature turns out to have been already furnished in the opening lines. The amplitude of the conversation slowly, steadily grows wider; mass scenes and throng images are introduced obliquely.

When Farinata stands up in his contempt for Hell like a great nobleman who has landed in prison, the pendulum of the conversation is already measuring the full diameter of the gloomy plain, broken by flames.

The notion of scandal in literature is much older than Dostoevsky, but in the thirteenth century and in Dante's work it was far more powerful.

Dante runs up against Farinata, collides with him, in an undesired and dangerous encounter exactly as the rogues in Dostoevsky are always blundering into their tormentors in the most inopportune places. From the opposite direction comes a voice—whose it is, is so far not known. It becomes harder and harder for the reader to conduct the expanding canto. This voice—the first theme of Farinata—is the minor Dantean *arioso* of the suppliant type, extremely typical of the *Inferno*.

O Tuscan, who travels alive through this city of fire and speaks so eloquently, do not refuse my request to stop for a moment. By your speech I recognize in you a citizen of that noble region to which I—alas!—was too great a burden.[10]

Dante is a poor man. Dante is an internal *raznochinets* [an intellectual, not of noble birth] of an ancient Roman line. Not courtesy but something completely opposite is characteristic of him. One has to be a blind mole not to notice that throughout the *Divina Commedia* Dante does not know how to behave, he does not know how to act, what to say, how to make a bow. This is not something I have imagined; I take it from the many admissions which Alighieri himself has strewn about in the *Divina Commedia*. The inner anxiety and the heavy, troubled awkwardness which attend every step of the unself-confident man, the man whose upbringing is inadequate, who does not know what application to make of his inner experience or how to objectify it in etiquette, the tortured and outcast man—it is these qualities which give the poem all its charm, all its drama, and they create its background, its psychological ground.

If Dante were to be sent out alone, without his *dolce padre*, without Vergil, a scandal would inevitably erupt in the very beginning, and we should not have a journey among torments and remarkable sights but the most grotesque buffoonery.

The gaucheries averted by Vergil systematically correct and straighten the course of the poem. The *Divina Commedia* takes us into the inner laboratory of Dante's spiritual qualities. What for us are an unimpeachable capuche and a so-called aquiline profile were, from the inside, an awkwardness overcome with torturous difficulty, a purely Pushkinian, Kammerjunker struggle[11] for the social dignity and social position of the poet. The shade that frightens old women and children was itself afraid, and Alighieri underwent fever and chills all the way from marvelous fits of self-esteem to feelings of utter worthlessness.

Up to now Dante's fame has been the greatest obstacle to understanding him and to the deeper study of him and it will for a long time continue to be so. His lapidary quality is nothing other than a product of the huge inner imbalance which found its outlet in the dream executions, the imagined encounters, the exquisite retorts, prepared in advance and nurtured by biliousness, calculated to destroy utterly his enemy, to bring about the final triumph.

How many times did the loving father, preceptor, sensible man, and guardian silence the internal *raznochinets* of the fourteenth century, who was so troubled at finding himself in a social hierarchy at the same time that Boccaccio, practically his contemporary, delighted in the same social system, plunged into it, sported about in it?

Che fai?—"What are you doing?"—sounds literally like the shout of a teacher: "You've gone crazy!" Then one is rescued by the playing of the organ pipes, which drown out shame and cover embarrassment.

It is absolutely incorrect to conceive of Dante's poem as a single narration extended in one line or even as a voice. Long before Bach and at a time when large monumental organs were not yet being built, and there existed only the modest embryonic prototypes of the future marvel, when the chief instrument was still the zither, accompanying the voice, Alighieri constructed in verbal space an infinitely powerful organ and was already delighting in all of its imaginable stops and inflating its bellows and roaring and cooing in all its pipes.

> Come avesse lo inferno in gran dispitto[12]
> (*Inferno*, X, 36)

—the line that gave rise to all of European demonism and Byronism. Meanwhile, instead of elevating his figure on a pedestal, as Hugo, for example, would have done, Dante envelops it in muted tones, wraps it about in grey half-light, hides it away at the very bottom of a dim sack of sound.

This figure is rendered in the diminuendo stop; it falls down out of the dormer window of the hearing.

In other words, the phonetic light has been switched off. The grey shadows have been blended.

The *Divina Commedia* does not so much take up the reader's time as intensify it, as in the performance of a musical piece.

In lengthening, the poem moves further away from its end, and the end itself arrives unexpectedly and sounds like a beginning.

The structure of the Dantean monologue, built on a system of organ stops, can be well understood with the help of an analogy to rocks whose purity has been violated by the intrusion of foreign bodies. Granular admixtures and veins of lava point to one earth fault or catastrophe as the source of the formation. Dante's lines are formed and colored in just such a geological way. Their material structure is infinitely more important than the famous sculptural quality. Let us imagine a monument of granite or marble the symbolic function of which is not to represent a horse or a rider but to disclose the inner structure of the very marble or granite itself. In other words, imagine a monument of granite which has been erected in honor of granite and as though for the revelation of its idea. You will then receive a rather clear notion of how form and content are related in Dante.

Every unit of poetic speech—be it a line, a stanza, or an entire composition—must be regarded as a single word. When we pronounce, for example, the word "sun," we are not throwing out an already prepared meaning—that would be a semantic abortion—we are living through a peculiar cycle.

Every word is a bundle and the meaning sticks out of it in various directions, not striving toward any one official point. When we pronounce "sun" we are, as it were, making an immense journey which has become so familiar to us that we move along in our sleep. What distinguishes poetry from automatic speech is that it rouses us and shakes us awake in the middle of a word. Then the word turns out to be far longer than we thought, and we remember that to speak means to be forever on the road.

The semantic cycles of Dante's cantos are so constructed that what begins with *mëd* "honey," for instance, ends with *med'* "bronze," and what begins with *lai*, "bark of a dog," ends with *lëd*, "ice."

Dante, when he has to, calls the eyelids "the lips of the eye." That is when the icy crystals of frozen tears hang from the lashes and form a covering which prevents weeping.

> gli occhi lor, ch'eran pria pur dentro molli,
>   gocciar su per le labbra, . . .[13]
>   (*Inferno*, XXXII, 46–47)

Thus, suffering crosses the organs of sense, creates hybrids, produces the labial eye.

There is not one form in Dante—there is a multitude of forms. One is driven out of another and it is only by convention that they can be inserted one into the other.

He himself says: "io premerei di mio concetto il suco" (*Inferno*, XXXII, 4), "I would squeeze the juice out of my idea, out of my conception." That is, form is conceived of by him as something wrung out, not as something that envelops. Thus, strange as it may be, form is pressed out of the content —the conception—which, as it were, envelops the form. Such is Dante's clear thought.

But only if a sponge or rag is wet can anything, no matter what, be wrung from it. We may twist the conception into a veritable plait but we will not squeeze from it any form unless it is in itself a form. In other words, any process of creating a form in poetry presupposes lines, periods, or cycles of form on the level of sound, just as is the case with a unit of meaning that can be uttered separately.

A scientific description of Dante's *Comedy*—taken as a flow, a current—would inevitably take on the aspect of a treatise on metamorphoses, and would strive to penetrate the multitudinous states of the poetic matter just as a physician making a diagnosis listens to the multitudinous unity of the organism. Literary criticism would approach the method of live medicine.

III.

Penetrating as best I can into the structure of the *Divina Commedia*, I come to the conclusion that the entire poem is one single unified and indivisible stanza. Or, to be more exact, not a stanza but a crystallographic shape, that is, a body. There is an unceasing drive toward the creation of form that penetrates the entire poem. The poem is a strictly stereometric body, one integral development of a crystallographic theme.

It is unthinkable that one might encompass with the eye or visually imagine to oneself this shape of thirteen thousand facets with its monstrous exactitude. My lack of even the vaguest notion about crystallography—an ignorance in this field, as in many others, that is customary in my circle—deprives me of the pleasure of grasping the true structure of the *Divina Commedia*. But such is the astonishing, stimulating power of Dante that he has awakened in me a concrete interest in crystallography, and as a grateful reader—*lettore*—I shall endeavor to satisfy him.

The formation of this poem transcends our notions of invention and composition. It would be much more correct to acknowledge instinct as its guiding principle. The approximate definitions offered here have been intended as anything but a parade of my metaphoric inventiveness. This is a struggle to make the whole conceivable as an entity, to render in graphic terms what is conceivable. Only with the aid of metaphor is it possible to find a concrete sign for the forming instinct with which Dante accumulated his terza rima to the point of overflowing.

Thus, one has to imagine how it would be if bees had worked at the creation of this thirteen-thousand-faceted shape, bees endowed with instinctive stereometric genius, who attracted more and still more bees as they were needed. The work of these bees, who always keep an eye on the whole, is not equally difficult at the various stages of the process. Their cooperation broadens and becomes more complex as they proceed with the formation of the combs, by means of which space virtually arises out of itself.

The analogy with bees, by the way, is suggested by Dante himself. Here are the three lines which open Canto XVI of the *Inferno*:

> Già era in loco ove s'udia il rimbombo
> dell'acqua che cadea nell'altro giro,
> simile a quel che l'arnie fanno rombo; . . .[14]
>   (*Inferno*, XVI, 1–3)

Dante's similes are never descriptive, that is, purely representational. They always pursue the concrete goal of giving the inner image of the structure or the force. Let us take the very large group of bird similes—all those long caravans now of cranes, now of crows, and now the classical military phalanxes of swallows, now the anarchically disorderly ravens, unsuited to Latin military formations—this group of extended similes always corresponds to the instinct of pilgrimage, travel, colonization, migration. Or let us take, for example, the equally extensive group of river similes, portraying the rise in the Apennines of the river Arno, which irrigates the Tuscan plain, or the descent into the plain of Lombardy of its alpine wet nurse, the river Po. This group of similes, marked by an extraordinary liberality and a step-by-step descent from tercet to tercet, always leads to a complex of culture, homeland, and unsettled civic life, to a political and national complex, so conditioned by water boundaries and also by the power and direction of rivers.

The force of Dante's simile, strange as it may seem, is directly proportional to our ability to get along without it. It is never dictated by some beggarly logical necessity. What, pray tell, could have been the logical necessity for comparing the poem as it neared its end to an article of attire—*gonna*, what we would today call a "skirt" but in early Italian meant, rather, a "cloak" or "dress" in general—and himself to a tailor who, forgive the expression, had run out of stuff?

IV.

As Dante began to be more and more beyond the powers of readers in succeeding generations and even of artists themselves, he was more and more shrouded in mystery. The author himself was striving for clear and exact knowledge. For his contemporaries he was difficult, he was exhausting, but in return he bestowed the award of knowledge. Later on, things got much worse. There was the elaborate development of the ignorant cult of Dantean mysticism, devoid, like the very idea of mysticism, of any concrete substance. There appeared the "mysterious" Dante of the French etching, consisting of a monk's hood, an aquiline nose, and some sort of occupation among mountain crags. In Russia this voluptuous ignorance on the part of the ecstatic adepts of Dante, who did not read him, claimed as its victim none other than Alexander Blok:

> The shade of Dante with his aquiline profile
> Sings to me of the New Life...[15]

The inner illumination of Dante's space by light—light derived from nothing more than the structural elements of his work—was of absolutely no interest to anyone.

I shall now show how little concern the early readers of Dante felt for his so-called mysteriousness. I have in front of me a photograph of a miniature from one of the very earliest copies of Dante, made in the mid-fourteenth century (from the collection in the library of Perugia). Beatrice is showing Dante the Holy Trinity. A brilliant background with peacock designs, like a gay calico print, the Holy Trinity in a willow frame—ruddy, rosy-cheeked, round as merchants. Dante Alighieri is depicted as an extremely dashing young man and Beatrice as a lively, round-faced girl. Two absolutely ordinary little figures—a scholar, exuding health, is courting a no less flourishing girl.

Spengler, who devoted some superlative pages to Dante, nevertheless saw him from his loge in a German *Staatsoper*, and when he says "Dante" one must nearly always understand "Wagner, as staged in Munich."

The purely historical approach to Dante is just as unsatisfactory as the political or theological. Future commentary on Dante belongs to the natural sciences, when they shall have been brought to a sufficient degree of refinement and their capacity for thinking in images sufficiently developed.

I have an overwhelming desire to refute the disgusting legend that Dante's coloring is inevitably dim or marked by the notorious Spenglerian brownness. To begin with, I shall refer to the testimony of one of his contemporaries, an illuminator. A miniature by him is from the same collection in the museum at Perugia. It belongs to Canto I: "I saw a beast and turned back." Here is a description of the coloring of this remarkable miniature, which is of a higher type than the preceding one, and completely adequate to the text.

> Dante's clothing is *bright blue* (*adzura chiara*). Vergil's beard is long and his hair is *grey*. His toga is also *grey*. His short cloak is *rose*. The hills are bare, *grey*.

Thus we see here bright azure and rose flecks in the smoky grey rock.

In Canto XVII of the *Inferno* there is a monster of transportation named Geryon, something like a super-tank, and with wings into the bargain. He offers his services to Dante and Vergil, having received from the sovereign hierarchy an appropriate order for the transportation of two passengers to the lower, eighth circle:

> Due branche avea pilose infin l'ascelle;
> > lo dosso e il petto ed ambedue le coste
> > dipinte avea di nodi e di rotelle:
> con più color, sommesse e sopraposte
> > non fer mai drappi Tartari nè Turchi,
> > nè fur tai tele per Aragne imposte.[16]
> > > (*Inferno*, XVII, 13–18)

The subject here is the color of Geryon's skin. His back, chest, and sides are gaily colored with decorations consisting of little knots and shields. A more brilliant coloration, Dante explains, is not to be found among the carpets of either Turkish or Tatar weavers.

The textile brilliance of this comparison is blinding, and nothing could be more unexpected than the drapery-trade perspectives which are disclosed in it.

In its subject, Canto XVII of the *Inferno,* devoted to usury, is very close to commercial goods assortments and banking turnover. Usury, which made up for a deficiency in the banking system, where an insistent demand was already being felt, was the crying evil of that time, but it was also a necessity which facilitated the circulation of goods in the Mediterranean world. Usurers were vilified in the church and in literature, but they were still resorted to. Usury was practiced even by noble families—odd bankers whose base was farming and ownership of land—and this especially annoyed Dante.

The landscape of Canto XVII is composed of hot sands—that is, something related to Arabian caravan routes. Sitting on the sand are the most aristocratic usurers: the Gianfigliazzi, the Ubbriachi from Florence, the Scrovigni from Padua. Around the neck of each there hangs a little sack or amulet, or purse embroidered with the family arms on a colored background: one has an azure lion on a golden background, a second has a goose whiter than freshly churned butter against a blood-red background, and a third has a blue pig against a white ground.

Before embarking on Geryon and gliding off into the abyss, Dante inspects this strange exhibit of family crests. I call your attention to the fact that the bags of the usurers are given as samples of color. The energy of the color epithets and the way they are placed in the line muffle the heraldry. The colors are named with a sort of professional brusqueness. In other words, the colors are given at the stage when they are still located on the artist's palette in his studio. And why should this be surprising? Dante knew his way around in painting, was the friend of Giotto, and closely followed the struggle of artistic schools and fashionable tendencies.

Credette Cimabue nella pittura[17]
(*Purgatorio*, XI, 94)

Having looked their fill at the usurers, they take their seats on Geryon. Vergil puts his arm around Dante's neck and says to the official dragon: "Descend in wide, flowing circles, and remember your new burden."

The craving to fly tormented and exhausted the men of Dante's time no less than alchemy. It was a hunger for cleaving space. Disoriented. Nothing visible. Ahead—only that Tatar back, the terrifying silk dressing gown of Geryon's skin. One can judge the speed and direction only by the torrent of air in one's face. The flying machine has not yet been invented, Leonardo's designs do not yet exist, but the problem of gliding to a landing is already solved.

And finally, falconry breaks in. The maneuvers of Geryon as he slows the rate of descent are likened to the return of a falcon who has had no success and who after his vain flight is slow to return at the call of the falconer. Once having landed, he flies off in an offended way and perches at an aloof distance.

Let us now try to grasp all of Canto XVII as a whole, but from the point of view of the organic chemistry of the Dantean imagery, which has nothing to do with allegory. Instead of retelling the so-called contents, we shall look at this link in Dante's work as a continuous transformation of the substratum of poetic material, which preserves its unity and strives to penetrate into its own interior.

As in all true poetry, Dante's thinking in images is accomplished with the help of a characteristic of poetic material which I propose to call its transformability or convertibility. It is only by convention that the development of an image can be called development. Indeed, imagine to yourself an airplane (forgetting the technical impossibility) which in full flight constructs and launches another machine. In just the same way, this second flying machine, completely absorbed in its own flight, still manages to assemble and launch a third. In order to make this suggestive and helpful comparison more precise, I will add that the assembly and launching of these technically unthinkable machines that are sent flying off in the midst of flight do not constitute a secondary or peripheral function of the plane that is in flight; they form a most essential attribute and part of the flight itself, and they contribute no less to its feasibility and safety than the proper functioning of the steering gear or the uninterrupted working of the engine.

It is of course only by greatly straining the meaning of "development" that one can apply that term to this series of projectiles that are built in flight and flit away one after the other for the sake of preserving the integrity of the movement itself.

The seventeenth canto of the *Inferno* is a brilliant confirmation of the transformability of poetic material in the above sense of the term. The figures of this transformability may be drawn more or less as follows: the little flourishes and shields on the varicolored Tatar skin of Geryon—silk, ornamented carpet fabrics, spread out on a shop-counter on the shore of the Mediterranean—maritime commerce, perspective of banking and piracy—usury—the return to Florence via the heraldic bags with samples of colors that had never before been in use—the craving for flight, suggested by the oriental ornamentation, which turns the material of the canto in the direction of the Arabian fairy tale with its device of the flying carpet—and, finally, the second return to Florence with the aid of the falcon, irreplaceable precisely on account of his being unnecessary.

Not satisfied with this truly miraculous demonstration of the transformability of poetic material, which leaves all the associative process of modern European poetry simply nowhere, and as if in mockery of his slow-witted reader, Dante, when everything has already been unloaded, used up, given away, brings Geryon down to earth and benevolently fits him out for new wanderings as the nock of an arrow sent flying from a bowstring.

V.

Dante's drafts have of course not come down to us. There is no possibility of our working on the history of his text. But it does not follow from this, of course, that there were no rough copies full of erasures and blotted lines and that the text hatched full grown, like Leda's brood from the egg or Pallas Athene from the brow of Zeus. But the unfortunate gap of six centuries, and also the quite forgivable fact of the nonextant original, have played us a dirty trick. For how many centuries now has Dante been talked and written of as if he had put down his thoughts directly on the finest legal parchment? Dante's laboratory—with this we are not concerned. What has ignorant piety to do with that? Dante is discussed as if he had had the completed whole before his eyes even before he began to work and had busied himself with the technique of moulage—first casting in plaster, then in bronze. At the very best, he is handed a chisel and allowed to carve or, as they love to say, "sculpt." Here they forget one small detail: the chisel very precisely removes all excess, and the sculptor's draft leaves no material traces behind, something of which the public is very fond. The very fact that a sculptor's work proceeds in stages corresponds to a series of draft versions.

Draft versions are never destroyed.

In poetry, in the plastic arts, and in art generally there are no ready-made things.

We are hindered from understanding this by our habit of grammatical thinking—putting the concept "art" in the nominative case. We subordinate the process of creation itself to the purposeful prepositional case, and our thinking is something like a little manikin with a lead heart who, having wavered about in various directions as he should and having undergone various jolts as he went through the questionnaire of the declension—about what? about whom? by whom? and by what?—is at the end established in the Buddhist, schoolboy tranquility of the nominative case. A finished thing, meanwhile, is just as subject to the oblique cases as to the nominative case. Furthermore, our whole doctrine of syntax is a very powerful survival of scholasticism, and when it is put into its proper subordinate position in philosophy, in the theory of cognition, then it is completely overcome by mathematics, which has its own independent, original syntax. In the study of art this syntactic scholasticism has the upper hand and hour by hour it causes the most colossal damage. In European poetry those who are furthest away from Dante's method and, to put it bluntly, in polar opposition to him, are precisely the ones who are called Parnassians: namely, Heredia, Leconte de Lisle. Baudelaire is much closer to him. Still closer is Verlaine, and the closest of all French poets is Arthur Rimbaud. By his very nature Dante shakes the sense and violates the integrity of the image. The composition of his cantos resembles the schedule of the air transport network or the indefatigable circulation of carrier pigeons.

Thus the conversation of the draft version is a law of the energetics of the literary work. In order to arrive at the target one has to accept and take account of the wind blowing in a different direction. This is also the rule for tacking in a sailing vessel.

Let us remember that Dante Alighieri lived at the time when navigation by sail was flourishing and the art of sailing was highly developed. Let us not disdain to keep in mind the fact that he contemplated models of tacking and maneuvering. Dante had the highest respect for the art of navigation of his day. He was a student of this supremely evasive and plastic sport, known to man from the earliest times.

Here I should like to call attention to one of the remarkable peculiarities of Dante's psyche: his dread of direct answers, occasioned perhaps by the political situation in that most dangerous, intricate, and criminal century.

While the whole *Divina Commedia*, as we have already shown, is a series of questions and answers, every direct utterance of Dante's is literally squeezed out of him through the midwifery of Vergil or with the help of the nursemaid Beatrice, and so on.

Inferno, Canto XVI. The conversation is carried on with that impassioned haste known only to prisons: to make use at all costs of the tiny moment of meeting. The questions are put by a trio of eminent Florentines. About what? About Florence, of course. Their knees tremble with impatience and they dread to hear the truth. The answer, lapidary and cruel, comes in the form of a cry. At this, even though he has made a desperate effort to control himself, even Dante's chin quivers and he tosses back his head, and all this is conveyed in nothing more nor less than the author's stage direction:

> Così gridai con la faccia levata.[18]
> (*Inferno*, XVI, 76)

Dante is sometimes able to describe a phenomenon in such a way that there is absolutely nothing left of it. To do this he makes use of a device which I should like to call the Heraclitean metaphor, with which he so strongly emphasizes the fluidity of the phenomenon and with such a flourish cancels it altogether that direct contemplation, once the metaphor has done its work, is really left with nothing to live on. Several times already I have had occasion to remark that the metaphoric devices of Dante surpass our notions of composition, since our critical doctrines, fettered by the syntactic mode of thinking, are powerless before him.

> When the peasant, climbing to the top of a hill
> At that time of the year when the being who lights the world
> Least conceals his face from us
> And the watery swarm of midges yields its place to the mosquitos,
> See the dancing fireflies in the hollow,
> The same one where he, perhaps, labored as a reaper and as a plowman;
> So with little tongues of flame gleamed the eighth circle,
> All of which could be surveyed from the height where I

had climbed;
And as with that one who revenged himself with the
    help of bears,
Seeing the departing chariot of Elijah,
When the team of horses tore headlong into the sky,
Looked with all his might but saw nothing
Save one single flame
Fading away like a little cloud rising into the sky
So the tongue-like flame filled the crevices of the graves
Stealing away the property of the graves, their profit,
And wrapped in every flame there lay hidden a sinner.[19]

                          (*Inferno*, XXVI, 25–42)

If you do not feel dizzy from this miraculous ascent, worthy of the organ of Sebastian Bach, then try to show what is here the second and what the first member of the comparison. What is compared with what? Where is the primary and where is the secondary, clarifying element?

In a number of Dante's cantos we encounter impressionistic prolegomena. The purpose of these is to present in the form of a scattered alphabet, in the form of a leaping, glistening, splashed alphabet the very same elements which, according to the rule of the transformability of lyric poetry, are later to be united into the formulas of sense.

Thus, in this introduction we see the infinitely light, brilliant Heraclitean dance of the swarm of summer midges, which prepares us to hear the solemn and tragic speech of Odysseus.

Canto XXVI of the *Inferno* is the most saillike of all the compositions of Dante, the most given to tacking, the best at maneuvering. For resourcefulness, evasiveness, Florentine diplomacy, and a kind of Greek wiliness, it has no equals.

We can clearly discern two basic parts of the canto: the luminous, impressionistic preparatory passage and the balanced, dramatic account by Odysseus of his last voyage, how he sailed out over the deeps of the Atlantic and perished terribly under the stars of another hemisphere.

In the free flowing of its thought this canto is very close to improvisation. But if you listen attentively, it will become clear that the poet is inwardly improvising in his beloved, cherished Greek, for which nothing more than the phonetics, the fabric, is furnished by his native Italian idiom.

If you give a child a thousand rubles and then leave him the choice of keeping either the small change or the notes, he will of course choose the coins, and by this means you can take the entire amount away from him by giving him a ten-kopeck piece. Precisely the same thing has befallen European Dante criticism, which has nailed him to the landscape of Hell as depicted in the etchings. No one has yet approached Dante with a geologist's hammer, in order to ascertain the crystalline structure of his rock, in order to study the particles of other minerals in it, to study its smoky color, its garish patterning, to judge it as a mineral crystal which has been subjected to the most varied series of accidents.

Our criticism says: distance the phenomenon from me and I can handle it, I can cope with it. For our criticism, what is "a longish way off" (Lomonosov's[20] expression) and what is knowable are practically the same thing.

In Dante the images depart and say farewell. It is difficult to make one's way down through the breaks of his verse with its multitude of leave-takings.

We have scarcely managed to free ourselves from that Tuscan peasant admiring the phosphorescent dance of the fireflies nor rid our eyes of the impressionistic dazzling from Elijah's chariot as it fades away into a little cloud, before the pyre of Eteocles has already been mentioned, Penelope named, the Trojan horse has slipped past, Demosthenes has lent Odysseus his republican eloquence, and the ship of old age is already being fitted out. Old age, in Dante's understanding of that term, is first of all breadth of mental horizon, heightened capacity, the globe itself as a frame of reference. In the Odyssean canto the world is already round.

It is a canto which deals with the composition of the human blood, which contains within itself the salt of the ocean.

The beginning of the voyage is in the system of blood vessels. Blood is planetary, solar, salty...

With every fiber of his being Odysseus despises sclerosis just as Farinata despised Hell.

> Surely we are not born for security like a cow, it cannot be that we will shrink from devoting the last handful of our fading senses to the bold venture of sailing westward, beyond the Gates of Hercules, there where the world, unpeopled, goes on?

The metabolism of the planet itself takes place in the blood, and the Atlantic absorbs Odysseus and sucks down his wooden ship.

It is unthinkable to read the cantos of Dante without aiming them in the direction of the present day. They were made for that. They are missiles for capturing the future. They demand commentary in the *futurum*.

Time, for Dante, is the content of history, understood as a single, synchronic act. And conversely: the content is the joint containing of time with one's associates, competitors, codiscoverers.

Dante is an antimodernist. His contemporaneity is inexhaustible, measureless, and unending.

That is why the speech of Odysseus, bulging like the lens of a magnifying glass, may be applied to the war of the Greeks and the Persians as well as to the discovery of America by Columbus, the bold experiments of Paracelsus, and the world empire of Charles V.

Canto XXVI, devoted to Odysseus and Diomed, is a splendid introduction to the anatomy of Dante's eye, so naturally adjusted for one thing only: the revelation of the structure of the future. Dante had the visual accommodation of birds of prey, unsuited to focusing at short range: too large was the field in which he hunted.

To Dante himself may be applied the words of the proud Farinata:

"Noi veggiam, come quei che ha mala luce"[21]
(*Inferno*, X, 100)

We, that is, the souls of sinners, are capable of seeing and distinguishing only the distant future, for which we have a special gift. The moment the doors into the future are slammed in front of us, we become totally blind. In this regard we are like one who struggles with the twilight and, able to make out distant objects, cannot discern what is near him.

The dance basis is strongly expressed in the rhythms of the terza rima of Canto XXVI. One is struck here by the high lightheartedness of the rhythm. The feet are arranged in the movement of the waltz:

> E se già fosse, non saria per tempo;
>   così foss' ei da che pure esser dee:
>   chè più mi graverà, com'più m'attempo.[22]
>   (*Inferno*, XXVI, 10–12)

For us as foreigners it is difficult to penetrate to the ultimate secret of an alien poetry. It is not for us to judge; the last word cannot be ours. But in my opinion it is precisely here that we find that captivating pliability of the Italian language, which only the ear of a native Italian can fully grasp. Here I am quoting Marina Tsvetaeva, who once mentioned "the pliability of Russian speech."

If you pay close attention to the mouth movements of a person who recites poetry distinctly, it will seem as if he were giving a lesson to deaf-mutes; that is, he works as if he were counting on being understood even without the sound, articulating each vowel with a pedagogic obviousness. And it is enough to see how Canto XXVI sounds in order to hear it. I should say that in this canto the vowels are agitated, throbbing.

The waltz is essentially a wavy dance. Nothing even faintly resembling it was possible in Hellenic or Egyptian culture, but it could conceivably be found in Chinese culture, and it is absolutely normal in modern European culture. (For this juxtaposition I am indebted to Spengler.) At the basis of the waltz there lies the purely European passion for periodic wavering movements, that same intent listening to the wave which runs through all our theory of light and sound, all our theory of matter, all our poetry and all our music.

VI.

Envy, O Poetry, the science of crystallography, bite your nails in wrath and impotence: for it is recognized that the mathematical combinations needed to describe the process of crystal formation are not derivable from three-dimensional space. You, however, are denied that elementary respect enjoyed by any piece of mineral crystal.

Dante and his contemporaries did not know geological time. The paleontological clock was unknown to them: the clock of coal, the clock of infusorial limestone, granular, gritty, stratified clocks. They whirled around in the calendar, dividing the twenty-four hours into quarters. The Middle Ages, however, did not fit into the Ptolemaic system: they took refuge there.

To biblical genetics they added the physics of Aristotle. The two poorly matched things were reluctant to knit together. The huge explosive power of the Book of Genesis (the idea of spontaneous generation) assailed the tiny little island of the Sorbonne from all quarters, and it would be no mistake to say that Dante's people lived in an antiquity completely awash in the present, like the earthly globe embraced by Tiutchev's ocean. It is difficult for us to imagine how it could be that things which were known to absolutely everyone —cribbed schoolboy's notes, things which formed part of the required program of elementary education—how it could be that the entire biblical cosmogony with its Christian supplements could have been read by the educated men of that time quite literally as if it were today's newspaper, a veritable special edition.

And if we approach Dante from this point of view, it will appear that he saw in tradition not so much its dazzling sacred aspects as an object which, with the aid of zealous reporting and passionate experimentation, could be used to good effect.

In Canto XXVI of the *Paradiso* Dante goes so far as to have a personal conversation with Adam—an actual interview. He is assisted by Saint John the Divine, author of the Apocalypse.

I maintain that every element of the modern method of conducting experiments is present in Dante's approach to tradition. These are: the deliberate creation of special conditions for the experiment, the use of instruments of unimpeachable accuracy, the demand that the result be verifiable and demonstrable.

The situation in Canto XXVI of the *Paradiso* can be described as a solemn examination in the surrounding of a concert and of optical instruments. Music and optics constitute the heart of the matter.

The fundamental antinomy of Dante's "experiment" consists of the fact that he rushes back and forth between example and experiment. Example is drawn out of the patriarchal bag of ancient consciousness only to be returned to it as soon as it is no longer required. Experiment, pulling one or another needed fact out of the purse of experience, does not return them as the promissory note requires, but puts them into circulation.

The parables of the Gospel and the little scholastic examples of the science taught in school—these are cereals eaten and done away with. But the experimental sciences, taking facts out of coherent reality, make of them a kind of seed-fund which is reserved, inviolable, and which constitutes, as it were, the property of a time that is unborn but must come. The position of the experimenter as regards factology is, insofar as he strives to be joined with it in truth, unstable by its very nature, agitated and awry. It resembles the figure of the waltz that has already been mentioned, for, after every half-turn on the extended toe of the shoe, the heels of the dancer may be brought together, but they are always brought together on a new square of the parquet and in a way that is different in kind. The dizzying Mephisto Waltz of experimentation was conceived in the *trecento* or perhaps even long before that, and it was conceived in the process of poetic formation, the undulating proceduralness, the transformability of the poetic matter—the most precise of all matter, the most prophetic and indomitable.

Because of the theological terminology, the scholastic grammar, and our ignorance of the allegory, we overlooked the experimental dances of Dante's *Comedy*; to suit the ways of a dead scholarship, we made Dante look more presentable, while his theology was a vessel of dynamics.

A sensitive palm touching the neck of a heated pitcher identifies its form because it is warm. Warmth in this case has priority over form and it is that which fulfills the sculptural function. In a cold state, forcibly divorced from its incandescence, Dante's *Comedy* is suitable only for analysis with mechanistic tweezers, but not for reading, not for performing.

> Come quando dall'acqua o dallo specchio
>   salta lo raggio all'opposita parte,
>   salendo su per lo modo parecchio
> a quel che scende, e tanto si diparte
>   dal cader della pietra in egual tratta,
>   sì come mostra esperienza ed arte.[23]
>   (*Purgatorio*, XV, 16–21)

"As a ray of sunlight that strikes the surface of water or a mirror reflects back at an angle corresponding to the angle of its fall, which differentiates it from a falling stone that bounces back perpendicularly from the ground—which is confirmed by experience and by art."

At the moment when the necessity of an empirical verification of the legend's data first dawned on Dante, when he first developed a taste for what I propose to call a sacred—in inverted commas—induction, the conception of the *Divina Commedia* had already been formed and its success intrinsically secured.

The poem in its most densely foliated aspect is oriented toward authority, it is most resonantly rustling, most *concertante* just when it is caressed by dogma, by canon, by the firm chrysostomatic word. But the whole trouble is that in authority—or, to put it more precisely, in authoritarianism—we see only insurance against error, and we fail to perceive anything in that grandiose music of trustfulness, of trust, in the nuances—delicate as an alpine rainbow—of probability and conviction, which Dante has at his command.

> Col quale il fantolin corre alla mamma—[24]
> (*Purgatorio*, XXX, 44)

thus does Dante fawn upon authority.

Many cantos of the *Paradiso* are encased in the hard capsule of an examination. In some passages one can even hear clearly the examiner's hoarse bass and the candidate's quavering voice. The embedding-in of a grotesque and a genre picture (the examination of a baccalaureate candidate) constitutes a necessary attribute of the elevated and *concertante* compositions of the third part. And the first sample of it is given as early as in the second canto of the *Paradiso* (in Beatrice's discussion of the origin of the moon's dark patches).

To grasp the very nature of Dante's intercourse with authoritative sources, that is, the form and methods of his cognition, it is necessary to take into account both the concertolike setting of the *Comedy*'s scholastic cantos and the conditioning of the very organs of perception. Let alone the really remarkably staged experiment with the candle and the three mirrors, where it is demonstrated that the return path of light has as its source the refraction of the ray, I cannot fail to note the conditioning of vision for the apperception of new things.

This conditioning is developed into a genuine dissection:

Dante divines the layered structure of the retina: *di gonna in gonna...*[25]

Music here is not a guest invited in from without, but a participant in the argument; or, to be more precise, it facilitates the exchange of opinions, coordinates it, encourages syllogistic digestion, extends premises, and compresses conclusions. Its role is both absorptive and resolvent—its role is a purely chemical one.

When you plunge into Dante and read with complete conviction, when you transplant yourself entirely onto the poetic material's field of action, when you join in and harmonize your own intonations with the echoings of the orchestral and thematic groups which arise incessantly on the pocked and shaken semantic surface, when you begin to perceive through the smoky-crystalline matter of sound-form the glimmerings embedded within, that is, the extra sounds and thoughts conferred on it not by a poetic but by a geologic intelligence, then the purely vocal, intonational, and rhythmic work gives way to a more powerful coordinating activity—to conducting —and, assuming control over the area of polyphony and jutting out from the voice like a more complex mathematical dimension out of a three-dimensional state, the hegemony of the conductor's baton is established.

Which has primacy, listening or conducting? If conducting is only a prodding of music which anyway rolls on of its own accord, what use is it, provided the orchestra is good in and of itself and displays an irreproachable *ensemble*? An orchestra without a conductor, that cherished dream, belongs to the same category of "ideals" of pan-European banality as the universal Esperanto language that symbolizes the linguistic *ensemble* of all mankind.

Let us consider how the conductor's baton appeared and we shall see that it arrived neither too late nor too soon, but exactly when it should have, as a new, original mode of activity, creating in the air its own new domain.

Let us hear about the birth or, rather, the hatching of the modern conductor's baton from the orchestra.

1732: Time (tempo or beat)—once beaten with the foot, now usually with the hand. Conductor—*conducteur—der Anführer* (Walther, *Musical Dictionary*).

1753: Baron Grimm calls the conductor of the Paris Opera a woodchopper because of his habit of beating time aloud, a habit which has reigned in French opera since the day of Lully (Schünemann, *Geschichte des Dirigierens*, 1913).

1810: At the Frankenhausen music festival, Spohr conducted with a baton rolled up out of paper, without any noise, without any grimacing (Spohr, *Selbstbiographie*).[26]

The birth of the conductor's baton was considerably delayed—the chemically reactive orchestra had preceded it. The usefulness of a conductor's baton is far from being its whole justification. The chemical nature of orchestral sonorities finds its expression in the dance of the conductor, who has his back to the audience. And this baton is far from being an external, administrative accessory or a *sui generis* symphonic police which could be abolished in an ideal state. It is nothing other than a dancing chemical formula that integrates reactions comprehensible to the ear. I also ask that it not be regarded a supplementary, mute instrument invented for greater clarity and to provide additional pleasure. In a sense, this invulnerable baton contains within itself qualitatively all the elements of the orchestra. But how does it contain them? It is not redolent of them, nor could it be. It is not redolent in the same way the chemical symbol of chlorine is not redolent of chlorine or the formula of ammonia or ammonium chloride is not redolent of ammonium chloride or of ammonia.

Dante was chosen as the theme of this talk not because I intended to concentrate on him as a means of learning from the classics and to seat him together with Shakespeare and Leo Tolstoy at a kind of *table d'hôte* in Kirpotin's manner, but because he is the greatest, the incontestible proprietor of convertible and currently circulating poetic material, the earliest and at the same time most powerful chemical conductor of a poetic composition that exists only in swells and waves, in upsurges and maneuverings.

VII.

Dante's cantos are scores for a special chemical orchestra in which, for the external ear, the most easily discernible comparisons are those identical with the outbursts, and the solo roles, that is, the arias and ariosos, are varieties of self-confessions, self-flagellations, or autobiographies, sometimes brief and compact, sometimes lapidary, like a tombstone inscription; sometimes extended like a testimonial from a medieval university; sometimes powerfully developed, articulated, and reaching a dramatic operatic maturity, such as, for example, Francesca's famous cantilena.

Canto XXXIII of the *Inferno*, which contains Ugolino's account of how he and his three sons were starved to death in a prison tower by Archbishop Ruggieri of Pisa, is encased in a cello timbre, dense and heavy, like rancid, poisoned honey.

The density of the cello timbre is best suited to convey a sense of expectation and of agonizing impatience. There exists no power on earth which could hasten the movement of honey flowing from a tilted glass jar. Therefore the cello could come about and be given form only when the European analysis of time had made sufficient progress, when the thoughtless sundial had been transcended and the one-time observer of the shade stick moving across Roman numerals on the sand had been transformed into a passionate participant of a differential torture and into a martyr of the infinitesimal. A cello delays sound, hurry how it may. Ask Brahms —he knows it. Ask Dante—he has heard it.

Ugolino's narrative is one of Dante's most significant arias, one of those instances when a man, who has been given a unique, never-to-be-repeated chance to be heard out, is completely transformed under the eyes of his audience, plays like a virtuoso on his unhappiness, draws out of his misfortune a timbre never before heard and unknown even to himself.

It must be remembered that timbre is a structural principle, like the alkalinity or the acidity of this or that chemical compound. The retort is not the space in which the chemical reaction occurs. This would be much too simple.

The cello voice of Ugolino, overgrown with a prison beard, starving and confined with his three fledgling sons, one of whom bears a sharp, violin name, Anselmuccio, pours out of the narrow slit:

> Breve pertugio dentro dalla muda[27]
> (*Inferno*, XXXIII, 22)

—it ripens in the box of the prison resonator—here the cello's fraternization with the prison is no joking matter.

Il carcere—the prison supplements and acoustically conditions the verbalizing work of the autobiographic cello.

Prison has played an outstanding role in the subconscious of the Italian people. Nightmares of prison were imbibed with the mother's milk. The *trecento* threw men into prison with an amazing unconcern. Common prisons were open to the public, like churches or our museums. The interest in prisons was exploited by the jailers themselves as well as by the fear-instilling apparatus of the small states. Between the prison and the free world outside there existed a lively intercourse, resembling diffusion—the process of osmosis.

Hence the story of Ugolino is one of the migratory anecdotes, a bugaboo with which mothers frighten children—one of those amusing horrors which are pleasurably mumbled through the night as a remedy for insomnia, as one tosses and turns in bed. By way of ballad it is a well-known type, like Bürger's *Lenore*, the *Lorelei*, or the *Erlkönig*.

In such a guise, it corresponds to the glass retort, so accessible and comprehensible irrespective of the quality of the chemical process taking place within.

But the largo for cello, proffered by Dante on behalf of Ugolino, has its own space and its own structure, which are revealed in the timbre. The ballad-retort, along with the general knowledge of it, is smashed to bits. Chemistry takes over with its architectonic drama.

"I' non so chi tu sei, nè per che modo
venuto se 'quaggiù; ma Fiorentino
mi sembri veramente quand' io t'odo.
Tu dei saper ch'io 'fui conte Ugolino."[28]
(*Inferno*, XXXIII, 10–13)

"I do not know who you are or how you came down here,
but by your speech you seem to me a real Florentine. You
ought to know that I was Ugolino."

"You ought to know"—*tu dei saper*—the first stroke on the
cello, the first out-thrusting of the theme.

The second stroke: "If you do not burst out weeping now,
I know not what can wring tears from your eyes."

Here are opened up the truly limitless horizons of com-
passion. What is more, the compassionate one is invited in as
a new partner, and already his vibrating voice is heard from
the distant future.

However, it wasn't by chance I mentioned the ballad:
Ugolino's narrative is precisely a ballad in its chemical make-
up, even though it is confined in a prison retort. Present are
the following elements of the ballad: the conversation be-
tween father and sons (recall the *Erlkönig*), the pursuit of a
swiftness that slips away, that is—continuing the parallel with
the *Erlkönig*—in one instance a mad dash with his trembling
son in arms, in the other, the situation in prison, that is, the
counting of trickling *tempi*, which bring the father and his
three sons closer to the threshold of death by starvation,
mathematically imaginable, but to the father's mind unthink-
able. It is the same rhythm of the race in disguise—in the
dampened wailing of the cello, which is struggling with all its
might to break out of the situation and which presents an
auditory picture of a still more terrible, slow pursuit, decom-
posing the swiftness into the most delicate fibers.

Finally, in just the way the cello eccentrically converses
with itself and wrings from itself questions and answers,
Ugolino's story is interpolated with his sons' touching and
helpless interjections:

"...ed Anselmuccio mio
disse: 'Tu guardi sì, padre: che hai?'"[29]
        (Inferno, XXXIII, 50–51)

"...and my Anselmuccio said:
'Father, why do you look so? What is the matter?'"

That is, the timbre is not at all sought out and forced onto the story as onto a shoemaker's last, but rather the dramatic structure of the narrative arises out of the timbre.

VIII.

It seems to me that Dante has carefully studied all speech defects, that he has listened to stutterers and lispers, to whiners and mispronouncers, and that he has learned a good deal from them.

So I should like to speak about the auditory coloring in Canto XXXII of the *Inferno*.

A peculiar labial music: *abbo, gabbo, babbo, Tebe, plebe, zebe, converrebbe*. As if a wet-nurse were taking part in the creation of the phonetics. Lips now protrude like a child's, now are distended into a proboscis.

The labials form a kind of "enciphered bass"—*basso continuo*, that is, the chordal basis of harmonization. They are joined by smacking, sucking, whistling dentals as well as by clicking and hissing ones.

At random, I pull out a single strand: *cagnazzi, riprezzo, quazzi, mezzo, gravezza*...

Not for a second do the tweakings, the smacking, and the labial explosions cease.

The canto is sprinkled with a vocabulary that I would describe as an assortment of seminary ragging or of the bloodthirsty taunting-rhymes of schoolboys: *cuticagna* ("nape"); *dischiomi* ("pull out hair, locks of hair"); *sonar con le mascella* ("to yell," "to bark"); *pigliare a gabbo* ("to brag," "to loaf").

With the aid of this deliberately shameless, intentionally infantile orchestration, Dante forms the crystals for the auditory landscape of Giudecca (Judas' circle) and Caina (Cain's circle).

> Non fece al corso suo sì grosso velo
> di verno la Danoia in Osteric,
> nè Tanai là sotto il freddo cielo,
> com'era quivi: chè, se Tambernic
> vi fosse su caduto o Pietrapana,
> non avria pur dall'orlo fatto cric.[30]
> (*Inferno*, XXXII, 25–30)

All of a sudden, for no reason at all, a Slavonic duck sets up a squawk: *Osteric, Tambernic, cric* (an onomatopoeic little word—"crackle").

Ice produces a phonetic explosion and it crumbles into the names of the Danube and the Don. The cold-producing draught of Canto XXXII resulted from the entry of physics into a moral idea: from betrayal to frozen conscience to the ataraxy of shame to absolute zero.

In tempo, Canto XXXII is a modern scherzo. But what kind? An anatomic scherzo that uses the onomatopoeic infantile material to study the degeneration of speech.

A new link is revealed here: between feeding and speaking. Shameful speaking can be turned back, is turned back to champing, biting, gurgling, to chewing.

The articulation of feeding and speaking almost coincide. A strange, locust phonetics is created.

> Mettendo i denti in nota di cicogna—
> (*Inferno*, XXXII, 36)[31]

—using their teeth like grasshoppers' mandibles.

Finally, it is necessary to note that Canto XXXII is overflowing with anatomical lustfulness.

"That same famous blow which simultaneously destroyed

the wholeness of the body and injured its shadow." There, too, with a purely surgical pleasure: "He whose jugular verte-bra was chopped through by Florence."

Di cui segò Fiorenza la gorgiera.[32]
(*Inferno*, XXXII, 120)

And further: "Like a hungry man who greedily falls on bread, one of them fell on another and sank his teeth into the place where the neck and the nape join."

Là 've il cervel si giunge con nuca.[33]
(*Inferno*, XXXII, 129)

All this jigs like a Dürer skeleton on hinges and takes us to German anatomy.

After all, a murderer is a bit of an anatomist.

After all, for the Middle Ages an executioner was a little like a scientific researcher.

The art of war and the trade of execution are a bit like a dissection amphitheater's antechamber.

IX.

The *Inferno* is a pawnshop where all the countries and towns known to Dante lie unredeemed. There is a framework for the very powerful structure of the infernal circles. It cannot be con-veyed in the form of a funnel. It cannot be represented on a re-lief map. Hell is suspended on the iron wires of urban egoism.

It is wrong to conceive of the *Inferno* as something volu-metric, as some combination of enormous circuses, deserts with burning sands, stinking swamps, Babylonian capitals and mosques heated to red-hot incandescence. Hell contains nothing, and it has no volume, the way an epidemic, an infec-tious disease, or the plague has none; it is like any contagion, which spreads even though it is not spatial.

Love of the city, passion for the city, hatred of the city—these are the material of the *Inferno*. The circles of hell are nothing but the Saturn rings of exile. For the exile his sole, forbidden, and forever-lost city is scattered everywhere—he is surrounded by it. I *should* say that the *Inferno* is surrounded by Florence. The Italian cities in Dante—Pisa, Florence, Lucca, Verona—these dear civic planets—are stretched out into monstrous circles, extended into belts, restored to a nebulous, gaseous state.

The antilandscape character of the *Inferno* constitutes as it were the condition of its graphic quality.

Imagine that grandiose experiment of Foucault's carried out not with a single pendulum, but with a multitude of crisscrossing pendulums. Here space exists only insofar as it is a receptacle for amplitudes. To make specific Dante's images is as unthinkable as to enumerate the names of those who took part in the migration of peoples.

> As the Flemish between Wissant and Bruges, fearing the sea's flood tide, erect dikes to force back the sea, and as the Paduans construct embankments along the quays of the Brenta out of concern for the safety of their cities and bays, and in expectation of spring which melts the snows of the Chiarentana (a part of the snowclad Alps)—such were these dams, albeit not so monumental, whoever the engineer who built them.[34]
>
> (*Inferno*, XV, 4–12)

The moons of the polynomial pendulum swing here from Bruges to Padua, teach a course in European geography, give a lecture on the art of engineering, on the techniques of city safety, on the organization of public works, and on the significance of the alpine watershed for national interests.

Crawling as we do on our knees before a line of verse, what have we retained from these riches? Where are its godfathers, where its zealots? What are we to do about our poetry, which lags so shamefully behind science?

It is frightening to think that the blinding explosions of present-day physics and kinetics were put to use six hundred years before their thunder sounded: there are no words to brand the shameful, barbaric indifference to them on the part of the sad compositors of ready-made meaning.

Poetic speech creates its tools on the move and in the same breath does away with them.

Of all our arts only painting, and at that only modern French painting, still has an ear for Dante. This is the painting which elongates the bodies of the horses approaching the finish line at the race track.

Whenever a metaphor raises the vegetable colors of existence to an articulate impulse, I remember Dante with gratitude.

We describe just what cannot be described, that is, nature's text brought to a standstill; and we have forgotten how to describe the only thing which by its structure yields to poetic representation, namely the impulses, intentions, and amplitudes of oscillation.

Ptolemy has returned by the back door! . . . Giordano Bruno was burned in vain!

While still in the womb, our creations are known to each and every one, but Dante's polynomial, multi-sailed and kinetically incandescent comparisons still retain the charm of that which has been told to no one.

Amazing is his "reflexology of speech"—the science, still not well established, of the spontaneous psycho-physiological influence of the word on the discussants, the audience, and the speaker himself, and also on the means by which he conveys the impulse to speech, that is, signals by light a sudden desire to express himself.

Here he approaches closest of all the wave theory of sound and light, he establishes their relationship.

As a beast, covered with a cloth, is nervous and shudders, and only the moving folds of the material betray its dissatisfaction, thus did the first created soul [Adam's]

express to me through the covering [of light] how pleas-
ant and joyous it was to answer my question.[35]

(Paradiso, XXVI, 97–102)

In the third part of the *Comedy* (the *Paradiso*) I see a gen-
uine kinetic ballet. Here we have all possible kinds of lumi-
nous figures and dances, all the way up to the clacking of
heels at a wedding feast.

Before me four torches burned and the nearest suddenly
came to life and became as rosy as if Jupiter and Mars
were suddenly to become birds and exchange their
plumage.[36]

(Paradiso, XXVII, 10–15)

It's odd, isn't it: a man, who intends to speak, arms himself
with a taut bow, lays up a supply of bearded arrows, prepares
mirrors and convex lenses, and squints at the stars like a tailor
threading a needle...

I have devised this composite quotation, which is drawn
from various passages in the *Comedy*, to bring into more em-
phatic relief the speech-preparatory strategies of Dante's poetry.

The preparation of speech is even more his sphere than the
articulation, that is, than speech itself.

Recall the marvelous supplication which Vergil addresses
to the wiliest of Greeks.

It is all arippling with the softness of the Italian diph-
thongs.

Those curly, ingratiating and sputtering flame-tongues of
unprotected lamps, muttering about the oiled wick...

"O voi, che siete due dentro ad un foco,
s'io meritai di voi mentre ch'io vissi,
s'io meritai di voi assai o poco."[37]

(Inferno, XXVI, 79–81)

Dante determines the origin, fate, and character of a man

by his voice, just as medical science of his time made diagnoses by the color of urine.

X.

He is brimming over with a sense of ineffable gratitude toward the copious richness which is falling into his hands. He has a lot to do: space must be prepared for the influx, the cataract must be removed from rigid vision, care must be taken that the abundance of outpouring poetic material does not trickle through his fingers, that it does not disappear into an empty sieve.

> Tutti dicean: *"Benedictus qui venis"*;
>   e, fior gittando di sopra e dintorno,
>   *"Manibus o date lilia plenis."*[38]
>   (*Purgatorio*, XXX, 19–21)

The secret of his scope is that not a single word of his own is introduced. He is set in motion by everything except fabrication, except inventiveness. Dante and fantasy—why this is incompatible! For shame, French romantics, you miserable *incroyables* in red vests, slanderers of Alighieri! What fantasy is there in him? He writes to dictation, he is a copyist, a translator. He is bent double in the posture of a scribe who squints in fright at the illuminated original lent him from the prior's library.

I think I forgot to say that a hypnotist's seance was a sort of precondition to the *Comedy*. This is true, but perhaps overstated. If one takes this amazing work from the viewpoint of written language, from the viewpoint of the independent art of writing, which in 1300 enjoyed equal rights with painting and music and was among the most venerated professions, then to all the earlier suggested analogies a new one can be added—writing down dictation, copying, transcribing.

Sometimes, very seldom, he shows us his writing tools: A

pen is called *penna*, that is, it participates in a bird's flight; ink is *inchiostro*, that is, belonging to a cloister; lines of verse are also called *inchiostri*, or are designated by the Latin scholastic *versi* or, still more modestly, *carte*, that is, an amazing substitution, pages instead of lines of verse.

And when it is written down and ready, there is still no full stop, for it must be taken somewhere, it must be shown to someone to be checked and praised.

To say "copying" is not enough—rather it is calligraphy at the most terrible and impatient dictation. The dictator, the taskmaster, is far more important than the so-called poet.

. . . I will labor a little more, and then I must show my notebook, drenched with the tears of a bearded schoolboy, to a most strict Beatrice, who radiates not only glory but literacy too.

Long before Arthur Rimbaud's alphabet of colors, Dante conjoined color with the full vocalization of articulate speech. But he is a dyer, a textile worker. His ABC is an alphabet of fluttering fabrics tinted with colored powders, with vegetable dyes.

> Sopra candido vel, cinta d'oliva
>   donna m'apparve, sotto verde manto,
>   vestita di color di fiamma viva.[39]
>   (*Purgatorio*, XXX, 31–33)

His impulses toward colors can be more readily called textile impulses than alphabetic ones. Color for him is displayed only in the fabric. For Dante the highest concentration of material nature, as a substance determined by its coloration, is in textiles. And weaving is the occupation closest to qualitativeness, to quality.

Now I shall attempt to describe one of the innumerable conductorial flights of Dante's baton. We shall take this flight as it is, embedded in the actual setting of precious and instantaneous labor.

Let us begin with the writing. The pen draws calligraphic

letters, it traces out proper and common nouns. A pen is a small piece of bird's flesh. Of course Dante, who never forgets the origin of things, remembers this. His technique of writing in broad strokes and curves grows into the figured flight of flocks of birds.

> E come augelli surti di riviera,
>   quasi congratulando a lor pasture,
>   fanno di sè or tonda o lunga schiera,
> si dentro ai lumi sante creature
>   volitando cantavano, e faciensi
>   or D, or I, or L, in sue figure.[40]
>   (*Paradiso*, XVIII, 73–78)

Just as the letters under the hand of the scribe, who is obedient to the one who dictates and stands outside literature, as a finished product, are lured to the decoy of meaning, as to an inviting forage, so exactly do birds, magnetized by green grass—now separately, now together—peck at what they find, now forming a circle, now stretching out into a line.

Writing and speech are incommensurate. Letters correspond to intervals. Old Italian grammar—just as our Russian one—is always that same fluttering flock of birds, that same motley Tuscan *schiera*, that is, the Florentine mob, which changes laws like gloves, which forgets by evening the decrees promulgated that same morning for the public welfare.

There is no syntax: there is a magnetized impulse, a longing for the stern of a ship, a longing for a forage of worms, a longing for an unpromulgated law, a longing for Florence.

XI.

Let us turn again to the question of Dantean coloring.

The interior of a mountain crystal, Aladdin's expanse concealed within it, the lanternlike, lamplike, the candelabralike suspension of the piscine rooms implicit within it—this is the best of keys to a comprehension of the *Comedy*'s coloring.

A mineralogical collection is a most excellent organic commentary to Dante.

I permit myself a little autobiographical confession. Black Sea pebbles, tossed up by the surf, were of great help to me when the conception of this talk was ripening. I consulted frankly with the chalcedony, the cornelian, crystallized gypsum, spar, quartz, etc. I understood then that a stone is a kind of diary of the weather, a meteorological concentrate as it were. A stone is nothing but weather excluded from atmospheric space and put away in functional space. In order to understand this, it is necessary to imagine that all geological changes and displacements can be resolved completely into elements of the weather. In this sense, meteorology is more basic than mineralogy: it encompasses it, washes over it, it ages and gives meaning to it.

The delightful pages which Novalis devotes to miners and mining make specific the interconnection of stone and culture and, by causing culture to grow like a rock formation, illumine it out of the stone-weather.

A stone is an impressionistic diary of weather, accumulated by millions of years of disasters, but it is not only the past, it is also the future: there is periodicity in it. It is Aladdin's lamp penetrating into the geologic murk of future times.

In combining the uncombinable, Dante altered the structure of time or, perhaps, the other way around: he was forced to resort to a glossolalia of facts, to a synchronism of events, names, and traditions separated by centuries, precisely because he heard the overtones of time.

The method chosen by Dante is one of anachronism, and Homer, who appears with a sword at his side, in company with Vergil, Horace, and Lucan, from the dim shadow of the pleasant Orphic choirs, where the four together while away a tearless eternity in literary discussion, is its best expression.

Evidences of the standing-still of time in Dante are not only the round astronomical bodies, but absolutely all things and all persons' characters. Anything automatic is alien to him. He is disdainful of causality: such prophecies are fit for bedding down swine.

> Faccian le bestie Fiesolane strame
>> di lor medesme, e non tocchin la pianta,
>> s'alcuna surge ancora nel lor letame.[41]
>>> (*Inferno*, XV, 73–75)

If I were asked bluntly, "What is a Dantean metaphor?" I would answer, "I don't know," for a metaphor can be defined only metaphorically—and this can be substantiated scientifically. But it seems to me that Dante's metaphor designates the standing-still of time. Its root is not in the little word *how*, but in the word *when*. His *quando* sounds like *come*. Ovid's rumbling is closer to him than the French eloquence of Vergil.

Again and again I turn to the reader and ask him to "imagine" something, that is, I resort to analogy, which has a single goal: to fill up the insufficiency of our system of definition.

So, imagine that the patriarch Abraham and King David, and all of Israel, including Isaac, Jacob, and all their kinsmen, and Rachel, for whom Jacob endured so much, have entered into a singing and roaring organ, as into a house with the door ajar, and have disappeared within.

And our forefather Adam with his son Abel, and old Noah, and Moses the giver and obeyer of the law had entered into it even earlier.

> Trasseci l'ombra del primo parente,
>> d'Abel suo figlio, e quella di Noè,
>> di Moisè Legista e ubbidiente;
> Abraam patriarca, e David re,
>> Israel con lo padre, e co' suoi nati,
>> e con Rachele, per cui tanto fe'.[42]
>>> (*Inferno*, IV, 55–60)

And after this the organ acquires the ability to move—all its pipes and bellows become extraordinarily agitated and, raging and storming, it suddenly begins to back away.

If the halls of the Hermitage should suddenly go mad, if the paintings of all schools and masters should suddenly break loose from the nails, should fuse, intermingle, and fill the air of the rooms with futuristic howling and colors in violent agitation, the result then would be something like Dante's *Comedy*.

To wrench Dante away from scholastic rhetoric is to render the whole of European civilization a service of no small importance. I hope centuries of labor will not be required for this, but only joint international efforts will succeed in creating a true anticommentary to the work of many generations of scholiasts, creeping philologues, and pseudobiographers. Lack of respect for the poetic material—which can be comprehended only through the performance of it, only by a conductorial flight—was precisely the reason for the general blindness to Dante, to the greatest master-manager of this material, to European art's greatest conductor, who by many centuries anticipated the formation of an orchestra adequate—to what?—to the integral of the conductor's baton.

Calligraphic composition realized by means of improvisation: such is the approximate formula of a Dantean impulse, taken simultaneously both as a flight and as something finished. His comparisons are articulated impulses.

The most complex structural passages of the poem are performed on the fife, on a birdcall. Almost always the fife is sent out ahead.

Here I have in mind Dante's introductions, released by him as if they were trial balloons.

> Quando si parte il giuoco della zara,
>   colui che perde si riman dolente,
>   ripetendo le volte, e tristo impara;

con l'altro se ne va tutta la gente:
    qual va dinanzi, e qual di retro il prende,
    e qual da lato gli si reca a mente.
Ei non s'arresta, e questo e quello intende;
    a cui porge la man più non fa pressa;
    e così dalla calca si difende.[43]

(*Purgatorio*, VI, 1–9)

When the dice game is finished, the loser in sad solitude replays the game, dejectedly throwing the dice. The whole crowd dogs the footsteps of the lucky gambler: one runs out ahead, one plucks at him from behind, one curries favor asking to be remembered; but fortune's favorite continues on, he listens to all alike, and by shaking hands, he frees himself from the importunate hangers-on.

And thus the "street" song of the *Purgatorio*—with its crush of importunate Florentine souls who desire gossip first, intercession second, and then gossip again—proceeds in the birdcall of genre, on the typical Flemish fife that became painting only three hundred years later.

Another curious consideration suggests itself: the commentary (explanatory) is an integral structural part of the *Comedy* itself. The miracle ship left the shipyard with barnacles sticking to it. The commentary is derived from the hubbub of the streets, from rumor, from hundred-mouthed Florentine slander. It is unavoidable, like the halcyon hovering behind Batiushkov's ship.[44]

There, there, look: old Marzzuco—how well he bore himself at his son's burial! A remarkably courageous old man.... And do you know, they were quite wrong to chop off the head of Pietro de la Broccia—they had nothing on him.... A woman's evil hand is implicated here.... By the way, there he is himself—Let's go up and ask.

Poetic material has no voice. It does not paint and it does not express itself in words. It knows no form, and by the same token it is devoid of content for the simple reason that it exists only in performance. The finished work is nothing but a calligraphic product, the inevitable result of the performing impulse. If a pen is dipped into an inkwell, the work created, stopped in its tracks, is nothing but a stock of letters, fully commensurate with the inkwell.

In talking of Dante, it is more proper to have in mind the generation of impulses and not the generation of forms: impulses to textiles, to sails, to scholastics, to meteorology, to engineering, to municipalities, to artisans and craftsmen, a list that could be continued ad infinitum.

In other words, the syntax confuses us. All nominative cases should be replaced by datives of direction. This is the law of reversible and convertible poetic material, which exists only in the performing impulse.

—Everything is here turned inside out: the substantive is the goal, and not the subject of the sentence. It is my hope that the object of Dante scholarship will become the coordination of the impulse and the text.

NOTES

1. Thus I cried with face uplifted

   (*Inferno*, XVI, 76)

2. Qual soleano i campion far nudi ed unti,
     avvisando lor presa e lor vantaggio,
     prima che sien tra lor battuti e punti...
                              (*Inferno*, XVI, 22–24)

   As champions, naked and anointed, were wont to do, spying
   their grasp and vantage, ere they came to blows and thrusts
   at one another...

3. And soothing spoke that speech which first delights father and
   mothers;
   .   .   .   .
   Would tell her household about the Trojans, and Fiesole, and
   Rome

   (*Paradiso*, XV, 122–123; 125–126)

4. In Russian, *zaum*, the term used by Khlebnikov and other
   Futurist writers to describe their experimental work.

5. Poi si rivolse, e parve di coloro
     che corrono a Verona il drappo verde
     per la campagna; e parve di costoro
   quegli che vince e non colui che perde.
                              (*Inferno*, XV, 121–124)

Then he turned back, and seemed like one of those who run for the green cloth at Verona through the open field; and of them he seemed like the one who wins, and not the one who loses.

6. Averroës, who made the great comment
                              (*Inferno*, IV, 144)

7. Might those people, who lie within the sepulchres, be seen?
                              (*Inferno*, X, 7–8)

8. Io avea già il mio viso nel suo fitto;
     ed ei s'ergea col petto e colla fronte,
     come avesse lo inferno in gran dispitto...
                              (*Inferno*, X, 34–36)

Already I had fixed my look on his; and he rose upright with breast and countenance, as if he entertained great scorn of Hell...

9. "And if," continuing his former words, he said, "they have learnt that art badly, it more torments me than this bed."
                              (*Inferno*, X, 76–78)

10. "O Tosco, che per la città del foco
      vivo ten vai così parlando onesto,
      piacciati di ristare in questo loco.
    La tua loquela ti fa manifesto
      di quella nobil patria natio,
      alla qual forse fui troppo molesto."
                              (*Inferno*, X, 22–27)

"O Tuscan! who through the city of fire goes alive, speaking, thus decorously; may it please you to stop in this place.
Your speech clearly shows you a native of that noble country, which perhaps I troubled too much."

11. Kammerjunker was an honorary position in the Russian imperial court commonly bestowed on a man when he was still in his teens. Nicholas I made Pushkin a kammerjunker when the poet was in his thirties; he resented the gesture.

12. As if he entertained great scorn of Hell

    (*Inferno*, X, 36)

13. Their eyes, which only inwardly were moist before, gushed at the lids

    (*Inferno*, XXXII, 46–47)

14. Already I was in a place where the resounding of the water, that fell into the other circle, was heard like the hum which beehives make . . .

    (*Inferno*, XVI, 1–3)

15. From Blok's poem "Ravenna."

16. He had two paws, hairy to the armpits; the back and the breast, and both the flanks, were painted with knots and circlets: never did Tartars or Turks make cloth with more colours, groundwork and broidery; nor by Arachne were such webs laid on her loom.

    (*Inferno*, XVII, 13–18)

17. Cimabue thought to hold the field in painting

    (*Purgatorio*, XI, 94)

18. Thus I cried with face uplifted

    (*Inferno*, XVI, 76)

19. Quante il villan, ch'al poggio si riposa,
    nel tempo che colui che il mondo schiara
    la faccia sua a noi tien meno ascosa,
    come la mosca cede alla zanzara,

vede lucciole giù per la vallea,
    forse colà dove vendemmia ed ara:
di tante fiamme tutta risplendea
    l'ottava bolgia, sì com' io m'accorsi,
    tosto ch'io fui là've il fondo parea.
E qual colui che si vengiò con gli orsi
    vide il carro d'Elia al dipartire,
    quando i cavalli al cielo erti levorsi,
chè nol potea sì con gli occhi seguire
    ch'ei vedesse altro che la fiamma sola,
    sì come nuvoletta, in su salire:
tal si movea ciascuna per la gola
    del fosso, chè nessuna mostra il furto,
    ed ogni fiamma un peccatore invola.

(Inferno, XXVI, 25–42)

As many fireflies as the peasant who is resting on the hill—at the
    time that he who lights the world least hides his face from us,
when the fly yields to the gnat—sees down along the valley,
    there perchance where he gathers grapes and tills:
with flames thus numerous the eighth chasm was all gleaming,
    as I perceived, so soon as I came to where the bottom
    showed itself.
And as he, who was avenged by the bears, saw Elijah's chariot at
    its departure, when the horses rose erect to heaven,—
for he could not so follow it with his eyes as to see other than
    the flame alone, like a little cloud, ascending up:
thus moved each of those flames along the gullet of the foss, for
    none of them shows the theft, and every flame steals a sinner.

20. Mikhail Vasilievich Lomonosov (1711–1765). A distinguished
    chemist, Lomonosov was also a poet, prosodist, grammarian,
    historian, and promoter of Russian handicrafts.

21. "Like one who has imperfect vision, we see the things"
                                                    (Inferno, X, 100)

22. And if it were already come, it would not be too early. If only it
    had come! since indeed it must be: for it will weigh the heavier
    on me as I grow older.
                                                    (Inferno, XXVI, 10–12)

23. As when a ray of light leaps from the water or from the mirror to the opposite direction, ascending at an angle similar to that at which it descends, and departs as far from the line of the falling stone in an equal space, even as experiment and science shows...

(Purgatorio, XV, 16–21)

24. With the trust with which the little child runs to his mother

(Purgatorio, XXX, 44)

25. fold on fold

26. A. Kars, *Istorija orkestrovki* [History of orchestration] (Muzgiz, 1932).

27. A narrow hole within the mew

(Inferno, XXXIII, 22)

28. "I know not who you may be, nor by what mode you have come down here; but, when I hear you, in truth you seem to me a Florentine.
You know that I was Count Ugolino..."

(Inferno, XXXIII, 10–13)

29. "...ed Anselmuccio mio disse: 'Tu guardi sì, padre, che hai?'"

(Inferno, XXXIII, 50–51)

"...And my little Anselm said: 'You look so, father, what ails you?'"

30. Never did the Danube of Austria make so thick a veil for his course in winter, nor the Don afar beneath the frigid sky, as there was here: for if Tambernic had fallen on it, or Pietra-pana, it would not even at the edge have given a creak.

(Inferno, XXXII, 25–30)

31. Sounding with their teeth like storks

(*Inferno*, XXXII, 36)

32. Whose gorge was slit by Florence

(*Inferno*, XXXII, 120)

33. There where the brain joins with the nape

(*Inferno*, XXXII, 129)

34. Quale i Fiamminghi tra Guizzante e Bruggia,
    tremendo il fiotto che ver lor s'avventa,
    fanno lo schermo perchè il mar si fuggia;
  e quale i Padovan lungo la Brenta,
    per difender lor ville e lor castelli,
    anzi che Chiarentana il caldo senta:
  a tale imagine eran fatti quelli,
    tutto che nè sì alti nè sì grossi,
    qual che si fosse, lo maestro felli.

(*Inferno*, XV, 4–12)

As the Flemings between Wissant and Bruges, dreading the
    flood that rushes towards them, make their bulwark to repel
    the sea;
and as the Paduans, along the Brenta, to defend their villages
    and castles ere Chiarentana feels the heat:
in like fashion those banks were formed, though not so high
    nor so large, the master, whoever it might be, made them.

35. Tal volta un aminal coperto broglia
    sì che l'affetto convien che si paia
    per lo seguir che face a lui l'invoglia;
  e similmente l'anima primaia
    mi facea trasparer per la coperta
    quant'ella a compiacermi venia gaia.

(*Paradiso*, XXVI, 97–102)

Sometimes an animal sways beneath a covering so that its im-
    pulse must needs be apparent, since what envelops it follows
    its movements;

and in like manner that first soul made appear through its covering with what elation it advanced to do me pleasure.

36. Dinanzi agli occhi miei le quattro face
  stavano accese, e quella che pria venne
  incominciò a farsi più vivace;
e tal nella sembianza sua divenne,
  qual diverrebbe Giove, se'egli e Marte
  fossero augelli, e cambiassersi penne.
  (*Paradiso*, XXVII, 10–15)

Before my eyes the four torches stood enkindled, and the one which had first approached me began to grow more living;
and such became in semblance as would Jupiter if he and Mars were birds and should exchange their plumage.

37. "O ye, two in one fire! if I merited of you whilst I lived, if I merited of you much or little, . . ."
  (*Inferno*, XXVI, 79–81)

38. All were saying: *"Benedictus qui venis"*; and, strewing flowers above and around, *"Manibus o date lilia plenis."*
  (*Purgatorio*, XXX, 19–21)

39. Olive-crowned over a white veil, a lady appeared to me, clad, under a green mantle, with hue of living flame . . .
  (*Purgatorio*, XXX, 31–33)

40. And as birds, risen from the bank, as though rejoicing together o'er their pasture, make themselves now a round, now a long flock,
  so within the lights the sacred creatures flying sang, and in their shapings made themselves now D, now I, now L.
  (*Paradiso*, XVIII, 73–78)

41. Let the beasts of Fiesole make litter of themselves, and not touch the plant, if any yet springs up amid their rankness . . .
  (*Inferno*, XV, 73–75)

42. He took away from us the shade of our First Parent, of Abel his
    son, and that of Noah; of Moses the Legislator and obedient;
    Abraham the Patriarch; David the King; Israel with his father
    and his children, and with Rachel, for whom he did so much;
                                                    (*Inferno*, IV, 55–60)

43. When the game of dice breaks up, he who loses stays sorrow-
    ing, repeating the throws, and sadly learns:
    with the other all the folk go away: one goes in front, another
    plucks him from behind, and another at his side recalls him
    to his mind.
    He halts not and attends to this one and to that: those to
    whom he stretches forth his hand press no more; and so he
    extracts himself from the crowd.
                                                    (*Purgatorio*, VI, 1–9)

44. Konstantin Batiushkov (1787–1855), a poet and contemporary
    of Pushkin's, as well as the subject of an admiring poem by
    Mandelstam. The allusion here is to Batiushkov's poem "Sha-
    dow of a Friend."

TITLE AND FIRST LINE INDEX

TITLES IN SERIES

J.R. ACKERLEY Hindoo Holiday
J.R. ACKERLEY My Dog Tulip
J.R. ACKERLEY My Father and Myself
J.R. ACKERLEY We Think the World of You
CÉLESTE ALBARET Monsieur Proust
DANTE ALIGHIERI The New Life
W.H. AUDEN (EDITOR) The Living Thoughts of Kierkegaard
W.H. AUDEN W. H. Auden's Book of Light Verse
HONORÉ DE BALZAC The Unknown Masterpiece *and* Gambara
MAX BEERBOHM Seven Men
ALEXANDER BERKMAN Prison Memoirs of an Anarchist
ADOLFO BIOY CASARES Asleep in the Sun
ADOLFO BIOY CASARES The Invention of Morel
CAROLINE BLACKWOOD Corrigan
CAROLINE BLACKWOOD Great Granny Webster
MALCOLM BRALY On the Yard
JOHN HORNE BURNS The Gallery
ROBERT BURTON The Anatomy of Melancholy
CAMARA LAYE The Radiance of the King
GIROLAMO CARDANO The Book of My Life
J.L. CARR A Month in the Country
JOYCE CARY Herself Surprised (First Trilogy, Vol. 1)
JOYCE CARY To Be a Pilgrim (First Trilogy, Vol. 2)
JOYCE CARY The Horse's Mouth (First Trilogy, Vol. 3)
BLAISE CENDRARS Moravagine
NIRAD C. CHAUDHURI The Autobiography of an Unknown Indian
ANTON CHEKHOV Peasants and Other Stories
RICHARD COBB Paris and Elsewhere
COLETTE The Pure and the Impure
JOHN COLLIER Fancies and Goodnights
IVY COMPTON-BURNETT A House and Its Head
IVY COMPTON-BURNETT Manservant and Maidservant
BARBARA COMYNS The Vet's Daughter
EVAN S. CONNELL The Diary of a Rapist
JULIO CORTÁZAR The Winners
ASTOLPHE DE CUSTINE Letters from Russia
LORENZO DA PONTE Memoirs
ELIZABETH DAVID A Book of Mediterranean Food
ELIZABETH DAVID Summer Cooking
MARIA DERMOÛT The Ten Thousand Things
ARTHUR CONAN DOYLE Exploits and Adventures of Brigadier Gerard
CHARLES DUFF A Handbook on Hanging
J.G. FARRELL Troubles
J.G. FARRELL The Siege of Krishnapur
M.I. FINLEY The World of Odysseus
EDWIN FRANK (EDITOR) Unknown Masterpieces: Writers Rediscover Literature's Hidden Classics